Giving Presentations

Jo Billingham runs training courses in presentation skills for individuals and groups, working with people as diverse as undergraduates and company executives, and organizations as diverse as manufacturing and financial services. She also runs a range of courses in written communications, and works as a freelance writer on a number of business communications.

One Step Ahead . . .

The *One Step Ahead* series is for all those who want and need to communicate more effectively in a range of real-life situations. Each title provides up-to-date practical guidance, tips, and the language tools to enhance your writing and speaking.

Series Editor: John Seely

Titles in the series

Acknowledgements

I would like to thank series editor John Seely for guiding my thoughts, and those colleagues, friends, and family who read the draft and made valuable suggestions: Adam Saturley for his overall comments, actor Sonya Raymond for her advice on voice, and Allison Ashman for her medical corrections. Thanks are also due to the dozens of nervous and uncertain presenters on training courses, who have been honest about their difficulties before setting out to improve in this most visible and vulnerable area. And most of all enormous gratitude to my husband, Norman Billingham, for his constant patience and support, as well as the scientific snippets that appear in this book.

Giving Presentations

Jo Billingham

Cartoons by Beatrice Baumgartner-Cohen

OXFORD
UNIVERSITY PRESS

OXFORD UNIVERSITY PRESS

Great Clarendon Street, Oxford OX2 6DP

Oxford University Press is a department of the University of Oxford.
It furthers the University's objective of excellence in research, scholarship,
and education by publishing worldwide in
Oxford New York
Auckland Bangkok Buenos Aires Cape Town Chennai
Dar es Salaam Delhi Hong Kong Istanbul Karachi Kolkata
Kuala Lumpur Madrid Melbourne Mexico City Mumbai Nairobi
São Paulo Shanghai Taipei Tokyo Toronto

Oxford is a registered trade mark of Oxford University Press
in the UK and in certain other countries

Published in the United States
by Oxford University Press Inc., New York

© Josephine Billingham 2003

British Library Cataloguing in Publication Data
Data available

Library of Congress Cataloging in Publication Data
Data available

ISBN 0-19-860681-8

10 9 8 7 6 5 4 3 2

Typeset by Footnote Graphics Ltd, Warminster, Wiltshire
Printed in the UK by Ashford Colour Press Ltd, Gosport, Hampshire

Contents

Introduction

Good news!
The book will help you to avoid creating the audience reaction commented on by Lord Birkett:

I do not object to people looking at their watches when I am speaking. But I strongly object when they start shaking them to make certain they are still going.

Lord Birkett, *Observer* (1960)

You have probably bought this book because you have a presentation to give. You may be completely new to presenting and feel you would like some guidance on basics such as:

- planning and structuring;

- using visual aids;

- using your body language to help you communicate;

- conquering your nervousness.

Or, you may be an experienced presenter who would like to:

- polish your skills;

- be confident that every presentation will go well;

- have some tips to make presenting easier;

- start to enjoy the prospect of giving a presentation.

This book will guide you through:

- what you should say;

- structuring your presentation;

- using memory aids to keep you on track;

- choosing and using visual aids;

- working with different room layouts.

Whether you are an experienced presenter or someone who is coming to the role fresh, you probably feel that you could do with some help with your 'performance' skills. Therefore, this book will also help you to make sure that:

- your voice carries well and is interesting;

- you involve and interest your audience;

- you stand, sit, and move appropriately;

- your props are in the right place at the right time.

How to use this book

This book is devised so that you can use it in different ways.

Slow and sure

If you are preparing to do a presentation, you may find the most useful approach to the book is to go through it carefully, following the recommended steps.

Flick and dip

If you do not have a particular presentation in mind, you may want to take a 'pick it up and put it down' approach. As the book is divided into small sections, you should find it easy to dip into it and add to your skills during spare moments.

When time is tight

Sometimes you may not have much time to work on a presentation. So, as well as offering you a stepped approach, there are plenty of tips and advice for presenters in a hurry.

Raising your performance

More advanced presenters will want to look at look at the 'Raising your performance' sections. You will find them at the end of many of the chapters.

Check it out

Finally, in Part B you will find a mass of checklists and ideas to help you at every stage of your presentation.

Old wisdom
The need to speak in public is as old as the human race.

Throughout this book you will find snippets of 'old wisdom' covering over 2,000 years of helpful advice.

See also Part B for helpful, time-saving checklists

1 | About presenting

What is a presentation?

People give presentations in all kinds of ways and situations, and for all sorts of reasons. A presenter could be:

- standing or sitting;

- talking to strangers, or people they know well;

- using notes, or talking 'off the cuff';

- presenting individually, or as part of a team;

- using visual aids, or speaking without them;

- taking questions, or speaking with interruptions.

The atmosphere might be highly formal, or extremely casual.

The audience might be just one person, a group of hundreds, or anything in between.

You are unlikely to be 'presenting' when describing your holiday to friends and using 'visual aids' in the form of photos. However, you will be presenting if you are giving similar information to one person, across a desk, to persuade them to support your plan to organize package tours to that same destination.

See Ch. 2, Preparing,
and Ch. 7, Giving
your presentation

The presenting which causes people most concern is having to stand and talk to a group of people. Even here, there are variations in the level of formality, and the extent to which the situation feels natural.

People often make presentations during meetings when, for example, a treasurer explains a club's finances, or on courses when students present their research findings or their thoughts on a topic. In such cases, the speakers are *almost* being themselves—but not quite. Friends and family would recognize that they are using their personality in a different way, perhaps by being more assertive and in control.

Other presentations are more like 'show business'. They begin with rousing music, use dramatic lighting, and are supported by a team of technicians. The presenter may use film, slides, dramatic gestures, and an automatic prompt system to help them appear to be speaking spontaneously.

Presentation is not acting, though some of the skills used by presenters are similar to those used by actors. These include the way you use your body, face, voice, personality, and the way you sense the audience's reaction and adapt to it. But actors take on the physical and vocal qualities of another person, and learn the script by heart. Acting is at one extreme of communicating, and conversation is at the other. Presentation is between the two because when presenting you are still 'you'.

1 About presenting

The recitor cannot be an actor, for that is a different art; but he must be a messenger, and he should be as interesting, as exciting, as are all that carry great news.

W. B. Yeats, *Literature and the Living Voice* (1906)

Being someone else

| acting |
| presenting |
| teaching/training |
| everyday conversation |

Being yourself

Although presenting may not feel natural, with practice you will appear perfectly natural to your listeners. You will be able to come across as the true you, rather than a completely different person. Of course, the trick is to learn to relax into your presentation, and that is what this book plans to help you do.

1 About presenting

Why do we give presentations?

We do presentations for all kinds of reasons. We may be asked to present to a prospective employer, to company customers, or as part of a course we are taking. Or, we may need to put information across to club members or an action group. But why would we decide to present, rather than send a written document? Whatever the circumstances a presentation has many advantages, both for the speaker and the audience.

Fact
Listening is a passive way of receiving information. When you present, you need to break through that passiveness and get the audience to engage with the information, and you.

It's two-way communication

Presenting allows immediate, two-way communication. People can ask questions, which helps you ensure they have the information they need, and allows them to check that they fully understand it.

You can assess reactions

One of the biggest advantages of a presentation is that you can often assess the audience's reactions and adapt what you are saying accordingly. For example, you may want to persuade people to think something, such as that sport is good for children. If you see your audience is agreeing with you, you can move on to your next point. If you see that the audience looks doubtful, you can say more, or inject more commitment and enthusiasm into the way you are presenting the information. That ability to be adaptable at the moment of communication doesn't exist with written communications.

See Ch. 4, Choosing and preparing visual aids; Ch. 7, Giving your presentation; Ch. 9, Presenting with visual aids

You can have visual impact

By using visual aids—including your own body language—you can add visual interest and impact to what you are saying.

10

You can introduce variety

Another advantage of presenting is that speakers can move between different forms of communication. You can start by talking, then take some questions, discuss issues, return to talking, project visual images, and so on. You can change between standing and sitting. For example, you might stand when you present information, to assert your authority, but sit down with your audience while you discuss issues. This varies the pace and style of communication and involves more of the audience's senses, though you will need to make sure that you don't introduce so much variety that your presentation becomes distracting.

See Ch. 7, Giving your presentation; Ch. 9, Presenting with visual aids; Ch. 10, Managing your presentation

Present

Take questions

Discuss

Present

Show slides

Present

Take questions

You can control the information

As a speaker you have control over the audience. People glance through written documents, skim some parts, skip others, jump around the text, and read the end first! With a presentation, the audience has to listen to the information in the order in which you give it. They may not listen all the time, but overall they have to follow your structure and not 'pick and choose' for themselves what they hear, and when.

People can get to know you

A frequent reason for asking someone to do a presentation is that it allows the audience to learn more about the speaker. Customers, colleagues, lecturers, and prospective employers all ask people to make presentations. This gives you a chance to show your good qualities, including:

■ how quickly you think;

■ that you can construct an argument for or against a point;

■ how well you can express your ideas;

■ your energy;

■ your enthusiasm;

■ your personality;

■ your commitment;

■ how well you work under pressure.

Employers and clients will also be able to assess:

■ the extent to which they believe or trust the speaker;

■ whether they feel they would like to work with them;

■ how well the speaker will fit the rest of the team.

And if they already know you

Even if you already know the audience, a presentation is a chance for them to get to see you in a different way. You will seldom have such an opportunity to speak for a prolonged period, without interruption, so your presentation is a good chance to show how well your thoughts are connected.

At colleges and internal job interviews, presentations are a chance to show yourself in a position of authority.

Genuine speech is the expression of a genuine personality... Wherever genuine speech is spoken, it creates community.

Northrop Fry, *The Well-tempered Critic* (1963)

Remember!
Presentations are a great chance to show people
• how good you are at your role
• how enthusiastic you are
• how committed you are to a project, product, or idea.

Types of presentation

At college or university

Students are often asked to make a presentation as part of their course work. This can be to share what they have discovered, perhaps the results of experiments, or what they found out about a particular author, work, or theory. Students are also asked to do presentations as an assessed part of their course. This helps to balance the marks, between those with good writing skills, and those who are stronger on speaking.

At interviews

Organizations are increasingly asking people to do a short presentation as part of the recruitment process. A presentation will help the organization to see the candidate's personality and how well they will get on with clients, customers, and colleagues. Presentations are also a chance to show how well you cope under pressure, and how good you are at 'thinking on your feet'.

In the workplace

A lot of workplace communication is through presentations. Many of these will be 'selling' a product or service to a prospective client, or 'selling' an idea to colleagues or managers.

At meetings

Finally, there are all the meetings that take place. You may need to present facts or persuade people to a course of action at a parent–teacher association, at work, at a council meeting, or at a sports-club event.

Overcoming apprehension

Many people don't like giving presentations. This dislike can express itself as anything from feeling slightly nervous to a dread which is so severe that people will go to any lengths to avoid having to present. This can mean that they don't apply for certain courses or jobs, or take part in organizations and committees, because these involve presenting.

The good news is that being nervous is natural, and as with any kind of fear, people feel it at different levels. Even better news is that nerves can be controlled and used to help you. That is what this book will help you do. But why do we feel so nervous?

It's an unfamiliar situation

When presenting, we are in an unfamiliar situation. If we are not used to public speaking we don't know what to expect. Even experienced speakers, such as teachers and lecturers, admit to being nervous sometimes. This is because every audience is different: they know that the reaction may not be the same as last time, so they have to be alert not only to what they are saying and doing, but also to how people are reacting. If you prepare correctly, even the unfamiliar can seem familiar.

You only get one chance

There could be a lot depending on the presentation, such as whether you get a job or promotion, the mark or grade for your course, or a positive decision from a client or committee. Each presentation is important—and you only get one 'go'. There's no time to sit back and think during a presentation, as there is when sitting an exam or writing a report. When you have to present, you *must* do your thinking beforehand.

Good news!
It's normal to feel nervous about giving presentations.

See Ch. 7, Giving your presentation, to find out why, as well as
- how to avoid feeling nervous
- how to disguise it when you do!

Better news!
Nerves can help your presentation. This book will help you arrive at that happy situation.

See Ch. 6, Rehearsing

Time matters

Another reason people feel worried when they have to give a presentation is that they know that they need to invest time in preparing and practising, and time is always in short supply. We are happy to put off preparing—as a way of pretending that it isn't really going to happen. And we realise we are asking a lot of the listeners, who must agree to be in a certain place at a certain time, for a certain amount of time, to listen to us.

People tell 'scare stories'

You may have noticed that when you have to do something you find unpleasant, such as going to the dentist, people tell you horror stories about their and their friends' experiences! The same is true of presentations: people love to tell you about the things they have seen go wrong; they seldom bother to point out that you have many qualities which good presenters need, such as a warm manner, a sound knowledge of your subject, or a clear voice.

Negative experiences haunt us

Of course, you may have had a bad experience yourself. Don't despair. Next time things will be different—a different audience, a different subject—and now you are more experienced than you were last time. Learn from what happened, and from this book. Then, concentrate on what you are going to do next time, not what happened last time.

We just get frightened

Some speakers forget what they are nervous about and start being afraid of being nervous! Just remember, a certain level of nerves is good, as we shall see later.

 Do!

get people to tell you about presentations they enjoyed giving or listening to, and what they liked about them.

 Don't!

listen to people who want to tell you about their terrible presentation experiences. If they insist on telling you, learn from it. Think, 'How would I deal with that situation?'

 Do!

get people who give good presentations to give you feedback.

 Don't!

assume that because your presentation went well last time, it will automatically go well this time.

 Do!

remember that if you have had a bad experience, next time will be better. Even if the audience and subject are the same, you will be more experienced.

Are they really hard?

With so many people finding presentations hard to do, you might wonder whether they really are that difficult.

In one sense they are hard—they are hard work. When you're presenting, you are like a juggler. You have lots of things all going on at the same time, and you need to get everything right to put in a good performance.

Before the presentation you need to have thought about and decided on:

- what you are going to say;

- the order you will say it in;

- how you will prompt yourself with reminders;

- whether you plan to use visual aids, and if so which ones you plan to use;

- what you want to do about questions;

- whether you will be giving people handouts, and if so when;

- whether you will stand, or sit;

- your preferred room layout;

- what you should wear.

During the presentation you will be thinking about:

- where you are standing;

- how you are standing;

- using your notes;

- using your visual aids;

- keeping your voice audible and interesting;

- keeping your audience listening and interested;

- gauging the audience's response.

 Do!

work at it.
Presenting is 20%
inspiration, and 80%
perspiration.

 Do!

remember, all
audiences are
different, and so you
will always need to
- prepare
- plan
- practise.

Good news!
This book will help
you deal with all
these aspects of
presenting.

What makes a good presentation?

Successful presentations usually involve a lot of behind-the-scenes effort, and a good deal of concentration and hard work while actually giving the talk. When you see an excellent presentation where the speaker just seems to chat informally, giving the impression that the whole event was made up of spur-of-the-moment thoughts, that is almost certainly not what really happened. The more spontaneous and natural a presentation seems, the more work the presenter is likely to have invested in it.

Top tip
Think absolutely everything through before you start.

This is because, for a presentation to be really successful, a number of very different elements have to all come together at the right moment—just as with an athlete who trains conscientiously to be at peak performance for a specific event.

To do a really good presentation, you need to get a number of elements to come together at the right moment.

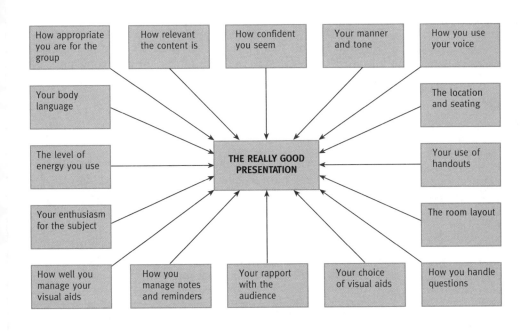

How appropriate you are for the group

How relevant the content is

How confident you seem

Your manner and tone

How you use your voice

Your body language

The location and seating

The level of energy you use

THE REALLY GOOD PRESENTATION

Your use of handouts

Your enthusiasm for the subject

The room layout

How well you manage your visual aids

How you manage notes and reminders

Your rapport with the audience

Your choice of visual aids

How you handle questions

2 | Preparing

✔ *Do!*

think about what the
people in the audience
could be like. This
includes their
● hopes
● fears
● ambitions
● knowledge
● prejudices
● opinions.

Picture this!
If speaking about an
artist you will want to
show their work, so
your starting point
may be the visual side
of your presentation.

Planning and preparing a presentation is a long journey and
your 'destination' is the really successful presentation. To make
sure you arrive at your destination, it's essential to invest time
in planning at the outset.

Start with some big questions

On the opposite page is a diagram of the main questions
you will need to ask yourself when preparing your
presentation. Although it looks complicated, many of the
questions are ones you would automatically ask yourself.
Others are points that presenters often overlook until the last
minute. Use the chart as the basis for building a strong and
appropriate presentation.

The order may vary

The order in which you ask the questions will depend on the
presentation you have to give. If talking to a club about your
favourite hobby, start with questions about the audience to
ensure your approach is appropriate for them. A talk to school
children about keeping rabbits would not be the same as a talk
on the same subject to retired people. If you are presenting to
your college group about your project, you would ask *why?*
before you think *who?* The answer might be:

> This presentation is to convince people that the paintings of
> Maes merit closer study.

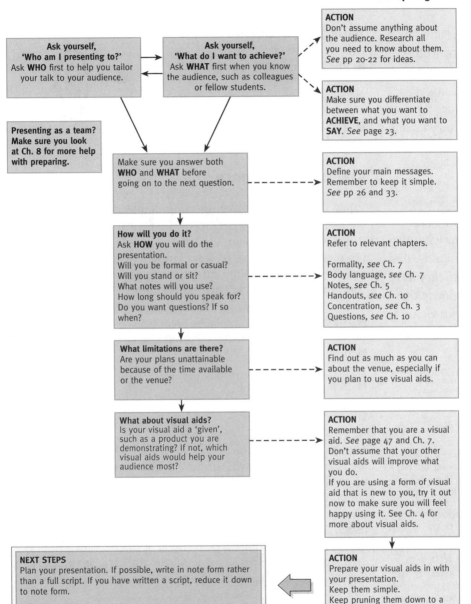

Ask yourself, 'Who am I presenting to?' Ask **WHO** first to help you tailor your talk to your audience.

Ask yourself, 'What do I want to achieve?' Ask **WHAT** first when you know the audience, such as colleagues or fellow students.

ACTION Don't assume anything about the audience. Research all you need to know about them. *See pp 20-22 for ideas.*

ACTION Make sure you differentiate between what you want to **ACHIEVE**, and what you want to **SAY**. *See page 23.*

Presenting as a team? Make sure you look at Ch. 8 for more help with preparing.

Make sure you answer both **WHO** and **WHAT** before going on to the next question.

ACTION Define your main messages. Remember to keep it simple. *See pp 26 and 33.*

How will you do it? Ask **HOW** you will do the presentation. Will you be formal or casual? Will you stand or sit? What notes will you use? How long should you speak for? Do you want questions? If so when?

ACTION Refer to relevant chapters.

Formality, *see Ch. 7* Body language, *see Ch. 7* Notes, *see Ch. 5* Handouts, *see Ch. 10* Concentration, *see Ch. 3* Questions, *see Ch. 10*

What limitations are there? Are your plans unattainable because of the time available or the venue?

ACTION Find out as much as you can about the venue, especially if you plan to use visual aids.

What about visual aids? Is your visual aid a 'given', such as a product you are demonstrating? If not, which visual aids would help your audience most?

ACTION Remember that you are a visual aid. *See page 47 and Ch. 7.* Don't assume that your other visual aids will improve what you do. If you are using a form of visual aid that is new to you, try it out now to make sure you will feel happy using it. See Ch. 4 for more about visual aids.

NEXT STEPS Plan your presentation. If possible, write in note form rather than a full script. If you have written a script, reduce it down to note form.

Rehearse, and then improve the content, your notes, and your visual aids. Rehearse, with audience feedback and using your visual aids. Rehearse at the venue, or a simulated venue.

ACTION Prepare your visual aids in with your presentation. Keep them simple. Keep pruning them down to a minimum.

| # Planning: the first steps

Top of your planning list is:

- know your audience

- know what you want to achieve

- define your key messages.

Know your audience

When you are communicating, you should always consider the audience—and particularly if you are giving a presentation. Why? When you present, you require people to be in a certain place, at a certain time, for a set amount of time. Respect them and their time by making sure that it is not wasted. They will want to hear something that they will find

- useful

- interesting

- important, or

- entertaining.

They may want just one of these qualities, several of them, or all of them. But they will certainly want *something* out of it. It's up to you to find out what it is, and provide it.

Also, if the content of a presentation is not right, the audience usually lets the speaker know! They may not challenge out loud, but may look bored, be restless, or fidget, which is distracting for the speaker. And, if the content is inappropriate, the speaker may fail to achieve what they set out to achieve.

You need to know:

- who they are AND why they are there.

He is one of those orators of whom it was well said, 'Before they get up, they do not know what they are going to say; when they are speaking, they do not know what they are saying; and when they have sat down, they do not know what they have said.'

Winston Churchill, talking about Lord Charles Beresford, House of Commons (1912)

Top tip
Think about your audience and what you want to *achieve*, rather than what you want to *say*. Then you'll be more likely to give a presentation, rather than a lecture!

Try this
I know this is familiar territory for some of you, but I would just like to introduce a few definitions for those who are new to the subject.

What do they know and think about the subject?

If your presentation is on the annual figures for your club, does your audience understand how net profit and gross profit are made up? Are some already familiar with what you need to say? If so, how can you make sure that they don't feel patronized or bored?

Do they have strong opinions on the subject?

Will they agree or disagree with what you are saying? Your audience may be overjoyed by the idea of a bypass around their village; or they may be dismayed. How many have which attitude? What are their objections?

Who is the decision maker?

If you want a decision, which person or people in the group is the decision maker? You may overlook people at the table who are very quiet and don't ask questions—but they may be the ones who decide who gets the job or contract.

What's in their minds?

Why are they there? What do they want to hear? What do they not want to hear? If you are telling people that the products will be in the UK on time, and the price has gone down, they will be pleased. If the product will be late, and the price has gone up, you have a different kind of presentation to give.

How many of them will be there?

Will there be a large group, or a small one? Will they expect you to stand on a stage, or at a lectern, or to sit at board table and present from there?

Who wants what?
If you're presenting a new work process, managers will want to know:
- the benefits
- costs
- downtime.

Other staff may be more interested in:
- the benefits
- training
- ease of use.

It's particularly important to tailor the content when you are presenting one-to-one.

What makes it [speech] worth uttering is not its truth ... but the fact of its being the one truth which is important in the present situation.

R. G. Collingwood, *The Principles of Art* (1938)

Do!

use a variety of communication methods—especially during long presentations. It will help to keep the audience interested.

Give your audience a chance to
- listen
- read
- talk/discuss/question
- handle papers or samples.

Top tip
Don't put on an act because you feel awkward about presenting to friends or colleagues. Just be yourself.

Try this
I know you have already heard . . . and I would like to reinforce . . . but I would like to offer an alternative view . . .

See Ch. 7, Giving your presentation, to find out how to project your personality

How long will they listen?

How long can this group concentrate on this subject? Young, new recruits may have low concentration spans for talks about pensions. Older staff might be happy to listen for longer.

What approach will interest them?

People have different preferences for receiving information. Some prefer listening; some like to discuss and share with others what they heard or read; others like strong visual elements. Some people like plain facts; some want points supported by detailed breakdowns of numbers; others like arguments with a strong 'people' element. Assess which will work best for the audience.

Are they willing, or grudging?

Is the audience there willingly, or have they been sent? What sacrifices have they made to be there? If they have been forced to give up a lunch break to listen to a presentation on health and safety they may not be overjoyed by the prospect.

Who else is speaking on a similar subject?

This happens in the workplace when several organizations are competing for a client or contract. Or at college a fellow student could give opinions or results exactly the opposite to your own. Think about how to handle this if it happens.

When you already know the audience

Some people find it hard to present to people they already know, such as committee members, colleagues, or fellow students. In this situation it's important to be yourself, and not to be glum if you are usually cheerful, or aloof if you are usually friendly.

Know what you want to achieve: your aim

The aim isn't about you. (*Your* aim is probably just to survive the whole presentation!) The aim is what you want to happen as a result of the presentation. It could be something you want people to do, such as offer you the job. Or, it could be something you want them to understand, such as how a new accounting process works. Or, it could be something you want them to believe or change their opinion about, such as the quality of a particular author or poet's work. No matter what you want to achieve, you must define it before you start preparing.

Once you have defined your aim, you will be able to:

■ omit any unnecessary or irrelevant details;

■ make sure that you are explicit, rather than expecting your audience to 'listen between the lines';

■ limit the number of points you make, by reducing the content to those which truly support your aim;

■ ensure your audience understands all steps in a process.

The strongest presentations are those in which the speaker makes just a few points, but reinforces them in a number of different ways.

Top tip
Write your aim on a piece of paper or card, and keep it in front of you all the time you are preparing your presentation. It will help you keep to the point.

Remember

Your aim is what you want people to

● do
● think
● believe
● agree to
● accept
● understand

| # Try a pattern diagram to stimulate ideas

A pattern diagram is a way of capturing your ideas and thoughts quickly. Many presenters find them useful for stimulating the brain about all aspects of a subject.

Try a pattern diagram when you want to:

■ see a point from all angles, to help you pre-empt tricky questions from the audience;

■ find new angles or content for over-familiar subjects;

■ find links between different aspects of a topic.

There are many other advantages to pattern diagrams.

■ All your ideas have equal value: you do not consider the first point you wrote is the most important, which we tend to do with conventional lists.

■ They are quick to do, and the more often you use them, the easier they get to do.

■ As all your ideas are on one sheet you can see links.

■ You can see where you need to do some research.

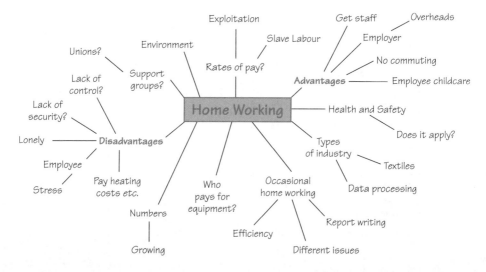

How to create a pattern diagram

1. Whenever you are creating a pattern diagram, try to work quickly and fluently, without interruptions.

2. Turn the paper so that you can use it in landscape format.

3. Write the subject of your presentation in the centre.

4. Think about your subject in detail—not just from your own point of view, but from the point of view of everyone who will be attending your presentation

5. As ideas come into your mind, draw lines from the centre, and write your ideas down on them.

6. Build out from the centre of the page. These are main headings and may become sections of your presentation.

7. Don't self-censor. Put down all your ideas and evaluate them later.

Try not to evaluate or reject ideas at this stage.

8. Use key words only—the words that will remind you of each idea. Use pictures if you prefer.

9. If one point or idea is closely connected to another, make it a branch off from the first point.

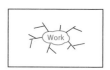

10. If you think ideas in different parts of the diagram are connected, use colour to show the connection. You can think about the connection in detail later.

11. After your first burst of ideas, return to your main headings and go into more detail. Really investigate the subject from all possible perspectives.

12. Keep branching out to give broad ideas at the centre of the page, and details towards the edge of the page.

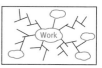

13. When your ideas slow down, go back round the map and see what else you come up with.

14. When it's time to stop doing your pattern diagram, draw round the different 'sections'. It will make it easier to follow.

Define your key messages

It's better to keep it simple than to have a complex calamity.

Support your point

Support your messages with:
- benefits
- examples
- facts
- figures
- research
- anecdotes or stories
- comparisons
- case histories.

Messages support aims. Messages are the reasons people should do what you want them to do, or think what you want them to think.

For example, if have to give a formal presentation as part of a job interview, your aim might be 'to get this job because I am desperate to get back into the workplace'! But you should state your message as: 'I have technical expertise, good people skills, and a lot of experience in managing budgets.'

Be selective

If you do a pattern diagram, you may find that you have far too much information to put across in your presentation. This is good. It means you have a richness of ideas, and you can now select just the best quality points to support your aim.

A common mistake that people make is to have too many messages. People simply will not remember seven or eight points. A presentation is far more effective if you make no more than three points, but support those points.

Aims and messages: how they work together

Your aim: I want to change the club's accounting procedures.

Your message: We need to change our accounting methods because the current processes were set up in 1952 and are no longer appropriate for the size or our membership, nor are they in line with modern accounting requirements. A new procedure will ensure that our funds are secure, that our methods are up to date, and will allow us to invest membership fees more profitably.

How will you give your presentation?

Once you have defined your audience, aim, and messages, it's time to start thinking about how you are going to do the presentation.

See Ch. 7, Giving your presentation, for more about nerves and visualization

There are many questions to ask yourself. Some of the answers may change as you continue your preparation. That doesn't mean that you should avoid them now. The more you can think and plan what you will be doing on the day, the more you will start to visualize yourself giving your presentation. Visualizing yourself presenting is a good way to:

■ help you overcome nerves;

■ make sure that nothing goes wrong on the day.

Many of these questions are dealt with in more detail in specific chapters.

See Ch. 3, Structuring

■ How long should the presentation be?

■ Should I stand, sit, or combine the two?

See Ch. 7, Giving your presentation

■ What will the room layout be like? Or can I choose the room layout?

See Ch. 10, Managing your presentation

■ Will the layout of the room limit me because of its size, shape, location of power points?

■ What advantages or restraints might the venue have?

■ Should I use handouts? If so, when should I distribute them?

■ Will I want questions? If so, would they be better at the end or as I go along?

See Ch. 4, Choosing and preparing visual aids

■ What about visual aids? Would they help me to achieve my aim? And if so, which ones should I use?

3 Structuring

Why structure?

One of the greatest fears people have about presentations is that they will get confused, miss things out, or repeat themselves. One way to prevent that happening is to have a sound structure. The structure helps you to move logically from one point to the next, so it is far less likely that you will leave out a whole section or point in your argument.

There are benefits from the point of view of your audience too. Most people find it more difficult to follow and remember information when they are listening, rather than reading. Your structure will help them to follow what you are saying—and when they can follow your argument, they are more likely to come to the same conclusion as you, or agree with your idea.

A three-part art

The overall shape of a presentation is, not surprisingly:

the beginning ➞ the middle ➞ the end

Each of these has its own, internal structure. In the case of 'the middle' there are several possible structures to choose from, or you may have to work out your own, unique structure.

Sound advice

The usual advice on presentations is:

↓

Tell them what you are going to tell them

↓

Tell them what you need to tell them

↓

Tell them what you just told them

This advice isn't only frequently offered. It's a good, sound presentation technique.

The beginning

The beginning is one of the two most vital parts of your presentation (the other is the ending). If you get the beginning wrong, you have missed an opportunity to embrace your audience. Stumble at this stage, and it sometimes takes a fair amount of time to recover your calmness.

See Ch. 7, Giving your presentation, to see how we form first impressions and how to use your voice

Opening comments

See Ch. 6, Rehearsing

It's appropriate to start with a general comment, perhaps about the weather, the stunning location, the traffic. This helps to establish a shared experience with the audience.

One reason for doing this is to help you make people warm to you, trust you, or accept you. Your first words are a chance to make people see that you are professional, confident, and know your subject. If you are telling your audience something they do not want to hear, you can at least appear understanding, sensitive to their feelings, and approachable.

Not a joking matter

Some people claim that it's good to start a presentation with a joke or humorous comment. Don't believe them! For most speakers this is bad advice. Jokes are usually about race, religion, nationality, sexuality, disability, death. Needless to say, jokes about such subjects are offensive. Even if you think you know your audience, you should not tell the joke. Don't even attempt a joke which doesn't offend anyone—even great stand-up comics sometimes tell jokes which go flat.

The same applies to humorous comments. There are few experiences so likely to throw you at the start of a presentation as saying something that is *meant* to be funny, and not getting the anticipated laugh.

At the start
Greet people
↓
Welcome them
↓
Thank them for attending
↓
Thank them for being punctual
↓
Comment on the weather, offices, room, traffic, or number of people there.

Introductions

Your name

The students you have been with every week for the last year will know it—so will your workmates and fellow committee members. But if there's anyone who does not know you, announce your name—clearly.

> Good morning—my name's Tom Adams.
>
> For those who do not already know me, my name is Tom Adams.

Your organization and authority

Build your audience's trust and respect by describing your connection with the subject.

> I am a third-year undergraduate in environmental science, and have been invited to talk to you about what life is like as a university student.

What they—and you—will be doing

This part of your presentation should answer the questions which are probably running through the minds of the audience:

- how long you will be speaking;

- whether they can interrupt or you will take questions at the end;

- whether there will be handouts, or they should take notes.

What's in a name?

Say your name clearly, with a tiny pause between your first and second names.

'My name is Janet ... King'

If you abbreviate and say your name too quickly, 'Jan King', the audience may think 'Is her name really Junking?'

If your presentation is part of the selection procedure for a job, your name is one thing you really want people to remember!

Use a standard structure or find a structure and stick to it. When preparing in a hurry, trying out new formats and creative structures can waste valuable time.

Your talk in outline

Your listeners will find it easier to follow your talk if you give an outline of what you will be covering.

> I will be talking about:
>
> ■ the academic side—how much work you are expected to do, and how it's different from school;
>
> ■ what it's like managing your money;
>
> ■ and the bit I'm sure you all want to hear about—the social side!

You may also need to . . .

If you are the first speaker on a day of presentations, or if you are the 'master of ceremonies', you may also need to mention:

■ fire precautions, including the different alarm sounds, location of the exits and the assembly points;

■ where the toilets are;

■ any refreshment breaks scheduled.

If some of the audience have heard the talk before

You may be asked to give a talk or presentation to a group of people, despite the fact that many of them may have already heard it, or the majority of its content. The most comfortable line to follow is to simply acknowledge the fact, in a positive way.

> I know this will be familiar information to some of you, but I hope you will find it a useful reminder and revision of facts that many people find they forget.

 Do!

listen to TV newscasters. They start: 'The main news stories tonight are . . .' Then they give you the news.

Part way through they tell you: 'The stories so far are . . .'

They end: 'Tonight's main stories are . . .'

The opening

Before starting the main part of your presentation cover:
● opening comment
● introductions (names)
● how long you will speak
● an outline of what's to follow
● when you want questions
● handouts.

Ding-a-ling

It may also be appropriate to ask people to turn off mobile phones.

And if something went wrong!

Occasionally, things may start badly. Perhaps the room has not been laid out as you expected, or the person with the keys cannot be found, the room is too cold, too hot, or the person next to you on the train poured coffee down your trousers.

Apologize—just once! If you can get it fixed, such as the heating, do so, and explain it's in hand. If the mark on your trousers won't show, don't mention it! (And definitely ignore rashes, blushes, and other quirks of your nerves!)

Putting the start together

> Good morning everyone. I'd like to start by saying what a pleasure it is to be inside these offices, which I have driven past every day for the last two years.
>
> My name is Janet King, and I'm here to give you a short talk about cricket, and what cricket has taught me that I believe would be useful to your organization. I'll be drawing on my experiences as a player in my school's first eleven, and as captain of my university team. The three areas I plan to cover are:
>
> ■ teamwork, including people management
> ■ energy
> ■ working under pressure.
>
> My talk will last about ten minutes, and then I'll be happy to answer any cricket questions you have. I'll be giving you a short handout at the end, but do make notes as well if you feel moved to take up cricket immediately!
>
> First of all, you might wonder why I became interested in cricket in the first place . . .

Once is enough
If things go wrong, one apology is enough—don't keep on about it and people will soon forget.

See Ch. 2, Preparing, and Ch. 10, Managing your presentation

Top tip
Learn your opening and close almost 'by heart' so that you can speak directly to your audience without referring to your notes (but have notes anyway—just in case!).

See Ch.5, Using notes

Structuring the middle

Recognize that people will 'drift off'

All audiences drift in and out of concentration: it's the way we listen. The audience's concentration will be highest at the start and end of your presentation.

Start ⟶ End

Concentration

He always hurries to the main event and whisks his audience into the middle of things as though they knew already.

Horace, *Ars Poetica* (65–8 BCE)

Keep it simple

Never forget, people find it much harder to follow and to remember spoken information. Some researchers believe our retention level for spoken information is as low as 20 per cent.

See Ch. 7, Giving your presentation

Use three whenever possible

People feel comfortable with things in groups of three, so break your talk into threes if you can: three arguments, three examples, three authors. If you have more than three, group them. For example, if you have five reasons why the company should offer you the job, look for three headings, with sub-points. Headings might be your people skills, your technical expertise, and your knowledge of the industry.

We like three

We hear groups of three when we are small . . .
- Hop, skip, and jump
- Reading, writing, and arithmetic
- Ready, steady, go

. . . and when we grow up
- Blood, sweat, and tears
- Education, education, education
- Hip, Hip, Hooray!

> *Did you know?*
>
> One of Churchill's famous speeches is often quoted wrongly? Although he said 'I have nothing to offer you but blood, toil, sweat, and tears', he is often quoted as saying only 'blood, sweat, and tears'.

'Deductive' or 'non-deductive'?

There are a number of traditional 'middles' to presentations which you can try. But the first decision you will need to make is whether your presentation lends itself to what is known as a *non-deductive* or a *deductive* structure. These complex-sounding terms are explained below.

The non-deductive approach

A *non-deductive* structure requires the audience to make discoveries while they are listening and to arrive at the conclusion themselves, rather than knowing the conclusion first and only looking to understand why it is true.

Fact + Fact + Fact + Fact *therefore* Conclusion

> The sky has been grey all morning, the wind is in the East where the weather has been wet for some time, and it's April which is traditionally a showery month. Therefore, I believe it will rain.

This is often used in detective fiction. It's interesting, but the reader or audience has to concentrate hard on what's being said.

The deductive approach

The *deductive* organization of material begins by giving the conclusion. This enables listeners to follow how the strands of arguments and points fit together.

Conclusion *because* Fact + Fact + Fact + Fact

> I believe it will rain because the sky has been grey all morning, the wind is in the East where the weather has been wet for some time, and it's April which is traditionally a showery month.

It is usually easier for listeners to follow the *deductive* structure so this is the one which presentations usually follow.

Whichever structure you use

- Keep it simple
- Use few facts
- Make a point, and then reinforce it in a variety of ways.

Remember

When you have a clear structure:
- you can keep on track of where you are
- your listeners can follow you
- it's easier to lead the audience to agree with you.

If appropriate do a shorter presentation and allow more time for questions.

Discursive presentations

To persuade people to a line of action or to agree with you, it can help if you present both sides of the argument. This way, they will feel they have been given a balanced view.

State your opinion:	We need to buy a school bus
▼	
The arguments for this need:	Less highway congestion; current car pollution; create safer school surroundings
▼	
The arguments against the bus:	Complaints from parents, inconvenience
▼	
The summing up:	The advantages outweigh the disadvantages

Alternatively, you can give the opposing view first. This can be useful as people often think about counter-arguments when someone is making a case for something.

Give the opposing position:	Parents need to feel their children are safely in school
▼	
State the problem:	However, cars on school premises cause congestion, pollution, and parking problems
▼	
Give your position:	I believe these cars also create a safety risk
▼	
Go through areas of agreement:	We all agree that safety is the prime concern
▼	
State the problem's resolution:	I believe we need a school bus

S—O—W the seeds for success

Remember!
Aim for three options.

This simple structure enables you to summarize the problem, the alternatives, and your own opinion in a very straightforward manner.

Situation: Parents' cars on site cause pollution, congestion, and are a safety hazard

▼

Options: Parents drop children outside the school (which they will not like)
Create a new entrance in North Road (but lose part of play area)
Get a mini-bus and pick up and drop children at appropriate points

▼

Way forward: Start process of obtaining mini-bus

Explaining processes

At college, on committees, and in the workplace, people often have to explain to a group of people how a process works. It could be anything from how a new security system for getting into the building operates, to a highly complex technique for doing an experiment, or how to use a piece of software.

Explain why before how
When explaining a process, it helps if you say what the end result will be.

'Now, I want to show you how you can transfer text from one document to another.'

See Ch. 4, Choosing visual aids

If you have to do this, the overall structure should always follow the order of the process. But:

■ give people a feel for how many steps are involved;

■ consider showing a diagram of the whole process at the start, and then go through the steps;

■ explain the point of each step of the process first;

■ use plenty of summaries;

■ allow opportunities to ask questions at each stage.

Make paragraph breaks clear

Readers have paragraphs to help them follow the sense of what they are reading. A paragraph break tells us that we are moving on to a new subject or point. Listeners do not have those breaks to help them follow what is being said. So, when you are speaking, you need to announce the paragraph breaks.

> I have told you something about Austen's use of irony. I would now like to go on to tell you a little about her use of metaphor.

Phrases for paragraphing
- This brings me to . . .
- I would now like to move on to . . .
- A connected point is . . .
- My next example . . .
- Following on from this . . .
- Firstly . . . Secondly . . .
- Let's now go on to consider . . .
- The next step . . .
- Another possibility . . .
- Moving on . . .

The ending

When people give presentations—particularly if they are new to them—they often overlook the importance of the end, and they trail off with a rather limp 'Well—that's all I've got to say, so—thank you'. What a missed opportunity!

The end of your presentation is your final chance to make your point. You should prompt your audience to do the thing that you decided you wanted them to do, whether that's reach a decision or change an attitude. Therefore, the end of the presentation has to be strong—and it needs just as much thought and effort as the opening.

Your performance has a lot to do with creating a strong ending, but the words are important too. So, as well as keeping your voice, face, and energy levels all up, you need to 'tell them what you just told them'.

Once you've announced the approaching end, don't run off at a tangent—or go through your whole presentation again. Just outline your main points, perhaps filling in a tiny bit more detail, and remind your audience of your message.

Introducing the end
- Finally . . .
- In conclusion . . .
- My last point . . .
- This brings me to . . .
- I would like to sum up by saying . . .
- And so to my closing point . . .
- Now that I am reaching the end of this talk, I would like to draw together . . .
- Lastly . . .
- I have one final observation . . .
- In summary . . .

Raising your performance

Until now, this chapter has covered the practical side of structuring your presentation: the principles, and how to deal with the start, the middle, and the end. But presenters often find that, once they have some experience and their confidence has grown, they want to be more adventurous.

Better beginnings

The start of your presentation is a good place to show your brilliance, and there are several techniques you may want to try.

Browse a bookshop

For presenters, bookshops are a rich source of material. Books of quotations, the greatest blunders, and *The Guinness Book of Records* are just a few examples of books that can trigger a brainwave.

> As Prime Minister David Lloyd George once said: 'Don't be afraid to take a big step if one is indicated. You can't cross a chasm in two small jumps.' I believe it's time for us to take that big step.

Work on it—and work it out

Think, consider, ponder, agonize . . . just keep working on it. Reflect on what people are saying about the product, the idea—or what's been said in the past. Consider staggering listeners with a statistic.

> Twenty years ago, around 609,000 IBM PCs and their clones were sold in one year. Now, manufacturers sell around half that number of PCs, *every day*.

Tip
If you do a lot of presentations, keep a 'scrap book' of bits and pieces that might help you bring the event to life, such as
- newspaper cuttings
- quotes from public figures
- cartoons and comic anecdotes.

Tip
Your audience may feel excluded if they have never heard of the person you quote, so avoid naming them.

'In 1957, it was said that data processing was a fad that wouldn't last a year!'

'It has been said that . . .'

'As a not-very-famous writer once said . . .'

Make it a current affair

Use recent articles, events, or trends as a starting or ending point, or the big news story that hit all the newspapers.

> You may have read recent newspaper articles claiming . . .

You can refer to a popular TV programme, or a pop song that you hear everywhere you go, if you are confident the audience will know what you are referring to. Such references really are 'of the moment' and even a few weeks later could seem out of date, but when they are well-chosen they work well.

Tell them what you're *not* going to tell them

You can cleverly tell people a lot, in brief, by telling them you are not going to tell them! This enables you to list a lot of points before going into detail about your chosen area.

> I am not going to tell you about the event I organized for 250 people with just two weeks' notice, nor about the brochure I produced which resulted in a 5% increase in membership. I'm not even going to tell you about the programme I ran for 12 newly-graduated recruits. Instead, I would like to tell you about . . .

Keeping the middle lively

Alliteration aids attention

Alliteration adds interest and polish to your presentation. Using alliterative words also helps people to remember what you said.

> We are introducing robust and responsible modern management.
>
> The software is fast, functional, and friendly.

Times change!
A few years ago grey-suited business executives everywhere were showing how up to date they were by announcing:

'I tell you what I want, what I really, really want . . .'

Anyone who tried that now would look decidedly behind the times.

Alliteration
Alliteration is using the same letter to begin a number of words in a stylish manner.

Similes and metaphors are apples of gold

Similes

Similes involve comparing one thing with another of a different kind:

Writing a book of poetry is like dropping a rose petal down the Grand Canyon and waiting for the echo.

E. Anthony, *O Rare Don Marquis*

Metaphors

Metaphors make comparisons by stating that a thing is the case, when it is not in a literal sense. The same example would read:

Writing a book of poetry is dropping a rose petal down the Grand Canyon and waiting for the echo.

Use similes and metaphors to bring a subject to life, but make sure they are original, and help you make a point.

> It's rather like sending your opening batsman to the crease only for them to find, the moment the first few balls are bowled, that their bats have been broken before the game—by the team captain.
>
> (Geoffrey Howe, following his resignation as Chancellor of the Exchequer, House of Commons, 1990)

Avoid being too complex. It's fine to say that running a company is like sailing a ship in a rough gale. Going on and on about navigation is irritating.

Be lively with language

> We are sleepwalking into a disaster.

Why not ask questions?

Ask rhetorical questions to help your audience stay awake by encouraging them to think. Simply ask the question you plan to answer, pause a moment, and begin your reply.

> Have you ever wondered why your runner beans don't flower? (*Pause*) Well, I have been looking into the wind pattern in this area and have found . . .

Paragraph by recognizing their needs

Acknowledge the fact that the subject is hard to follow.

> I promise I will bring all these arguments together later, but let's leave that one dangling there for now.

Paragraph by announcing the next subject

You can pause, and then announce the subject of the next section in a word or two. You need to be a confident speaker, and able to use your voice well, to make this technique work.

> ... and we expect these figures to be repeated in France, Italy and Spain.
>
> **Now for Germany!**
>
> In Germany, we are not expecting to see the kinds of changes that we have seen in France, Italy, and Spain. . .

Tip
When moving to a new point, use your voice to enable your listeners to 'hear' the headings—the parts which would be bold and underlined in a written document.

See Ch. 7, Giving your presentation

Ending with style

Remember, the end of your presentation is where you remind the audience of what you want them to think, do, or believe. If you are too 'clever' at the end, your audience may remember your technique more than your message. However, here are some you may want to try.

Pose a question

Use this only if you want to be controversial and challenging.

> Do we really want to go on in this way?
>
> Can this club really afford not to modernize its procedures?

Don't clap too hard—it's a very old building.

John Osborne, *The Entertainer* (1957)

Tell a story

If your presentation is fairly light in mood, you can end with a story or anecdote—but it should reinforce your message.

> Finally, I would just like to tell you about an incident that took place in the building on Tuesday morning . . .

4 Choosing and preparing visual aids

Important!

See also Ch. 7, Giving your presentation, and Ch. 9, Presenting with visual aids

Surprise!
You are your most important visual aid. To find out why see Ch. 7, Giving your presentation.

What are 'visual aids'?

The term 'visual aids' covers everything that you add to your presentation, which does not involve speaking. There are all kinds of ways you can do this. Some of the most popular are:

- PowerPoint

- whiteboards or blackboards

- 35 mm slides

- flip charts

- overhead projectors (OHPs).

Do we really need them?

The great speeches by public figures do not involve visual aids. They are memorable because they were spoken with passion, used language creatively, and captured a moment. It is hard to speak with conviction and emotion when you are led by visual aids. They control the content and the order, and tend to set the pace of the presentation. This means that if a particular audience, at a particular moment, needs the information presented differently, you have little flexibility to make changes.

Another problem with visual aids is that many speakers misuse them. Visual aids should *aid* a presentation—not be a substitute for it. They should be used to *reinforce* a message, not as a safeguard in case the speaker fails to make something clear. Visual aids should also be *visual* and, as we shall see later, *words* are not *visual*.

There are other negative aspects to visual aids.

- They can completely overpower speakers who are not lively and confident.

- They can cause all sorts of performance problems so it is essential to spend even more time rehearsing.

- Many visual aids are time-consuming to prepare—and doing them well takes longer. This often reduces valuable rehearsal time.

- The more complex and technical the visual aids are, the more there is to go wrong.

- Despite the assurances of people at the venue, the promised equipment may be unsuitable, or not compatible, or it may not be there after all!

However, visual aids do enable you to

- involve more senses: listeners look, as well as listen;

- show a process, for example by using a flow chart;

- help people to understand and recall figures;

- let listeners see what you are talking about, such as a painting, some scientific equipment, or fire damage;

- save time on explanations;

- make abstract ideas, such as trends, more concrete;

- change the stimulus and help concentration;

- create memorable images in the mind.

Know what's expected
If you are presenting to clients or if your presentation is part of a employee selection procedure, you may be expected to use visual aids.

Extra marks
College courses which are assessed partly on a presentation often award extra marks for the use of visual aids.

 Do!
always check the room before deciding which visual aids to prepare. Its size, shape, and the location of power supplies, could all limit your choice.

Keep it simple

Decide how many visual aids you need. With PowerPoint and slides aim for no more than one visual every two minutes.

 Do!

Before deciding which type of visual aids you will use, make sure you look at Ch. 9, Presenting with visual aids, to make sure you'll feel comfortable performing with them.

■ Make sure each visual has a heading.

■ Have no more than one idea to each visual.

■ Keep each visual uncluttered.

Words are not visual

If you show people text and talk to them at the same time they will not know whether to read or listen. Few brains can do both simultaneously. Most people will only take in part of what they see, and part of what they hear.

Never put up the words, and then read them to the audience. If you are tempted to do this—or told to do so by someone else— ask, what is the point? As your audience can read, why put yourself to the trouble of doing a presentation? You might as well just send them the presentation by post or e-mail.

Think mottoes and slogans

People remember slogans, mottoes, clever combinations of words. They are likely to remember three points (particularly if they all begin with the same letter) but may well forget some things if you give them five points. Fewer words will have more impact.

Environmental Policy

We have consistently shown an environmental policy which is:
■ fully co-ordinated with our other activities
■ constantly improves with time
■ adopts a range of new and innovative measures

Our Environmental Policy

■ Integrated
■ Improving
■ Innovative

Be visible

Normal typescript put onto a slide, PowerPoint screen, or overhead foil will normally not be visible. With some rooms even the people in front row will not be able to read it, and the people at the back of the room will be irritated, or doze off.

You could give people a glimpse of what a form or page of a magazine looks like—so long as they are not expected to read it. For legibility, in most rooms the type sizes need to be around twenty or twenty-two.

Remember
Your audience is there for a presentation. Not to watch you read to them.

Ariel 20 Univers 22

To make visual aids easy to read, use a typeface which does not have tiny projections at the end of each character. The projections are called 'serifs' and the unembellished typefaces are 'sans serif'. Sans serif typefaces, as used in the headings throughout this book, are easier to read on projected material.

Serif

Serif   Serif

Ariel and Univers are two of the most popular sans serif typefaces.

Pictures are better than words

Pictures are more memorable than words, so use a picture whenever you can. It does not have to be a photograph—even a simple hand-drawn sketch can have far more impact than text.

One picture is worth ten thousand words.

Frederick R. Barnard,
Printers' Ink (1927)

We care

When dealing in numbers

For many audiences, numbers in presentations have the potential to be boring. Mostly, people do not want numbers, but the story the numbers tell. They want interpretation, not the figures. So, ask yourself:

*Know your
audience*
Some audiences will
absorb numbers
more quickly than
others. Accountants,
engineers, and
physicists may like
more detail.

> How much numerical information do they want or need?

Provide the amount of information which is needed to help people understand your message, or to make an informed decision. More numbers will merely confuse your audience.

Round figures

Remember
People need to be
able to take in
numerical
information at a
glance.

When it is feasible to do so, round the figures up or down. But note, this may not always be acceptable to your audience.

Complex	Easier	Simple
£698,762.84	£699,000	almost £700,000

See Part B for a
recommended book
on presenting
numerical
information

Get in shape

One of the best ways to present numbers is to show the shape the figures create. Graphs, bar charts, and pie charts stay in the mind in a way mere numbers do not.

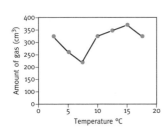

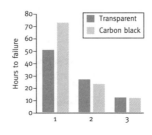

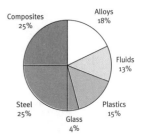

Colours

Colours

Use strong, dark colours, with bright, clear colours as highlights.

 Do!

think of yourself as your most important visual aid.

For visuals shown in a dark room, pale colours (yellow, white, pastels) on a dark background are easier to read. For those shown in light rooms (overhead projectors) use a dark colour on a clear background.

Use colours consistently throughout your presentation. Our brains sort information by colour and people may be confused if you keep changing them.

Choose colours which are appropriate to your environment. Blues and muted highlights are normal in business. Fluorescent colours and colour 'clashes' will be more suitable for younger audiences and more creative environments; pastels create a soft and caring impression, but are often not visible when projected.

Roughly 4 per cent of the population is colour blind, with red/green colour blindness the most common. Do not create visuals which rely on the distinction between, for example, the red and green figures.

Finally, never forget *you!*

It's worth noting here that you are always using at least one visual aid: *you!* And you are your most important visual aid.

See Ch. 7, Giving your presentation, to find out why your appearance is so important

Your 'body language' can either assist you or hinder you in your presentation. If you look positive and committed, people are more likely to trust you and agree with your messages. If you look miserable and half-hearted, people will be less likely to see your message in a positive light, no matter how good your other visual aids are.

PowerPoint

PowerPoint has almost taken over the business world as the way to do presentations, and is increasingly becoming part of the academic world as well. Despite that, people on the receiving end of such presentations constantly say how dull they found the experience. Also, more and more presenters are giving presentations with PowerPoint, disliking the experience, and saying 'never again!'

This is not the fault of PowerPoint: in both cases it's the fault of the presenter, who probably spent more time than intended on preparing the slides, and not enough on other aspects of the presentation. PowerPoint has enormous potential to lift a presentation—so long as it is used properly.

The advantages

■ PowerPoint is slick and highly professional.

■ Screens change at the click of the mouse.

■ If you have a remote control, you can move about the room or performance area as much as you want.

■ Your slides cannot get out of order.

■ You can reach any size audience, using multi-screens if necessary.

■ You can show photos of art, events, or people.

■ You can do interesting things such as fading pictures and bringing text in from different directions.

■ You can add sound and clips of video.

■ The presentation is compact and easy to carry.

■ You can distribute your presentation before or after your talk via e-mail, or make it available on the Web.

Disadvantages

Unfortunately, many of the points which are advantages to PowerPoint can become disadvantages if it is poorly used.

You may not be able to use PowerPoint at the venue. This could be due to the location of power supplies, incompatible technologies, or lack of appropriate connectors.

Do not be tempted to use the PowerPoint option which allows you to create slides of bullet points. Look at the other possibilities, and remember that words are not visuals.

Presenters who use lists of bullet points as prompts tend to keep looking at the screen behind them, or at the laptop.

In some rooms, you need to turn the light off for the screen to be clearly visible, so you and the audience are in the dark. You cannot see their reactions: in the dark, they could be dozing!

Even if you can see reactions, you have no flexibility to change the presentation while speaking, except by skipping slides. That makes audiences wonder what you omitted—and why.

People attempt to use all the clever facilities which PowerPoint offers. They pull in text from different directions, fade slides, and use sound effects. This can cause the audience to think about the techniques, rather than the message.

When to use PowerPoint

Choose PowerPoint when:

■ the audience expects it—as in client presentations—or you want to appear slick;

■ you want to show film, video clips, or photos;

■ you want to show graphs, charts, and other diagrams.

Don't be deadly dull
Many business presentations can be described by the term 'death by bullet point'.

Warning!
Remember what works with *your* technology may not work at another venue. For example, a presentation prepared with 'old' software may get automatically updated when you start presenting, causing an unexpected delay.

Safety net
Always have a fall-back position. Too much can go wrong to risk presenting without a safety net. For example, print your presentation on transparencies for use on an overhead projector.

49

Preparing a presentation with PowerPoint

Did I wake you?
A dark room, a dull subject, and a tedious voice are excellent conditions for inducing an unscheduled 'power nap'.

See pages 44–7 for guidance on colours and the content of the screens, and Part B for a recommended book on PowerPoint

PowerPoint can be projected onto a traditional, or 'active' screen. You can change the slides with an attached, or remote, mouse. The remote may be pointed at the terminal, the screen, or a projector, which may be suspended from the ceiling. If you use an 'active' screen—a kind of electronic whiteboard—you can also change screens by tapping the board.

Once you have prepared your presentation, go though it and ask yourself honestly how much the PowerPoint really adds. Reject anything that is simply serving as your notes, and keep on reducing the number of screens when you rehearse.

Consider using PowerPoint for just part of the presentation, such as a heading as you move from one section to the next. This can help you—and the audience—to focus on where you are in the presentation.

Work on the principle of telling, then showing. If you do this, you will speak for a time, and then summarize your points by showing them on screen. This creates some variety, and keeps your audience concentrating on *you*.

Remember, PowerPoint comes into its own for the truly visual: photos, organization charts, graphs.

Keep it simple. Do not be tempted to use all the clever things PowerPoint can do. A little, done well, is more effective.

Fact
Used well, PowerPoint can lift a good presentation to an excellent one. Used wrongly, it can reduce a good presentation to an hour of boredom.

Use blank slides, so that you do not have to leave something showing when you have finished talking about it.

If you want to refer to a screen more than once, put in a duplicate screen, rather than flicking back and forth through the presentation.

See page 107 on how to present with PowerPoint

Whiteboards and blackboards

Schools and colleges have whiteboards and blackboards you can use. They are more laborious to write on than flip charts (though they are also cheaper) and can slow down your presentation.

Warning!
Chalk dust goes everywhere!

Electronic whiteboards

These are whiteboard-sized and are part computer screen, part whiteboard. You can project your presentation on to them, and change your PowerPoint screen by tapping them. You can also write on them, and as they are touch sensitive, you can move text around on them. Some print off what you write on them, or you can create a disc to capture the notes.

They can be 'erratic' so only use one after plenty of practice.

Important
Always use the right kind of pen on whiteboards, or they will never come clean.
Take your own pens and chalk, and a board cleaner.

35 mm slides

Slide marking tradition
Mark slides in bottom left

Slides have almost disappeared in favour of PowerPoint and they share many of its advantages and disadvantages. However, they have better resolution than PowerPoint so use them if the detail of the image counts, for example if you are showing works of art. Lecturers in fine arts usually use slides.

- Stick a 'spot' in the bottom left of the slide frame.

- Number the spots on the slides.

- Load with the spot top right and facing the screen.

- Make an aluminium foil slide to create a dark screen.

- If you need to refer to a slide more than once, put a duplicate slide at the appropriate place to avoid having to go backwards and forwards through the slides.

Off the wall!
Wall-fixed flip charts can force you to stand a long way from your audience. Find out if a free-standing one will be available.

Write on
- Use black or blue
- Highlight with bright colours
- Letters about 5 cm height.

Tip
If you are preparing pages in advance, you can stick things on them, such as newspaper clippings.

Flip charts

Advantages

The possibility of using a flip chart is sometimes overlooked by presenters, yet they can have enormous advantages.

They can be used for groups of up to 40, depending on the size and shape of the room. You are not restricted by power sockets so can stand where you want in relation to the group.

You are not controlled by prepared visuals, so can avoid going through some points, or you can do more on others.

You can use the chart as a shared notepad: writing down ideas from the audience helps them to feel involved.

People watch information appear gradually, rather than seeing it all at once. This helps when presenting complex figures, such as the calculation of a 1/80th final salary (FS) pension after 18 years' service (Y), on a salary of £25,000 a year.

$$1/80th \times Y \times FS = \frac{18}{80} \times £25,000 = £5,625 \ a \ year$$

The flip chart keeps the focus on *you*. It is not as big and overwhelming as a large screen, and you can use natural light.

Other advantages are that:

■ they are relatively cheap;

■ not much can go wrong;

■ most venues can supply one.

'Here's one I did earlier'

You can write your flip chart pages in advance, but keep the pages flat. Wavy, creased paper looks messy and unprofessional.

Ghosting

4 Choosing and
preparing visual aids

You can 'ghost' things onto the chart. This involves writing in faint pencil which the audience cannot see, and going over it with pen during the presentation. It's very impressive to watch a perfect 'freehand' map of the United Kingdom appear.

If you do 'ghost' something, make sure that you mark the page. It is unnerving to find yourself writing all over the carefully laid out organization chart which you spent half an hour preparing to fit the page.

Disadvantages

There are of course disadvantages to flip charts as well.

They do not work well in all rooms as the writing may not be visible to people at the far end of a long room.

Their cheapness can be a disadvantage. Some sectors of business might consider them inappropriate.

You need reasonably good handwriting, and spelling. Weak spellers need to be careful if asking for ideas from a group. You may need to write up 'diarrhoea'!

When to use a flip chart

Choose to use a flip chart when you want:

■ an informal atmosphere

■ flexibility

■ a high level of involvement with your audience.

Tip
If you prepare pages in advance, leave a blank sheet between pages to prevent the writing showing through.

Sad fact
Flip chart enthusiasts are still hoping someone will invent a pen which contains a spell checker!

Poor spelling can be
embarassing ✗
embarrasing ✗
embarrassing ✓

Poor spelling?
● Abbreviate
● Make light of it
● Learn words you may need beforehand.

See page 108 for how to present with a flip chart, and Part B for a recommended book to help you with your spelling

Overhead Projectors (OHPs)

Advantages

While overhead projectors have almost disappeared from many types of presentations, they are still much-loved by many academics and teachers. This is partly because they work well when you are speaking to groups of hundreds, or to just a handful of people.

One great advantage of the OHP is that many places which do not have facilities for other visual aids, such as scout huts and church halls, can find a projector which you can use. They also give you some physical freedom—you can stand or sit, move around the room, and use natural light.

OHP slides (or foils) are usually prepared in advance, and normally typed, word-processed, or computer generated. You can also write or draw by hand, and you can even do this during your presentation, to highlight points—but be careful about smudging wet ink.

You can get plastic binders for acetates. This makes them easier to handle during performance. Also, if you want to write on your overhead while you are presenting, the binder can be wiped clean for 'repeat performances'.

Preparing foils

You can produce foils from word processors or PowerPoint, or write them by hand. They can be printed from the machine, or photocopied. Choose the right foil for the production method. Photocopiers and laser printers will melt certain foils.

See page 45 for advice on type size

Tip
Use a light background. Dark backgrounds use up an enormous amount of printing ink, which can make OHPs expensive.

Tip
Avoid using odd foils you find in the stationery cupboard. It could be an expensive 'economy'.

Disadvantages

Although OHPs are useful, they do have disadvantages, and in some businesses they would be considered old-fashioned.

The OHP is often badly positioned, on an uneven surface, or the glass may be grubby or scratched.

They are fiddly to work with. There are the foils you are yet to show, the one you are showing, and the ones you have shown. If you have interleaved the slides with sheets to stop them sticking to each other, you will also have a stack of paper.

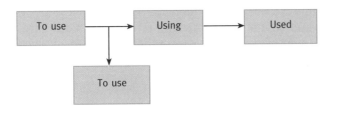

Tip
If you are using OHPs, make sure you number them. Then, if you drop them at the last minute, you're less likely to get in a flap.

It takes a moment to ensure the overhead is straight, and they can slide or get knocked while you are speaking.

It can be tricky to make sure that everyone can see the screen and, as you need to stay near the machine to change foils, it's easy for the speaker to block sight lines too.

They can get out of order, and your search for a foil, for example when answering a question, is visible to everyone.

When to use an OHP

Use an OHP:

■ when you want a down-to-earth feeling and suspect the audience would find other visual aids too slick;

See also page 109 for how to present with an OHP

■ when other alternatives are not available;

■ as a back-up to other forms of visual aid.

Raising your performance

Props

Props are anything you take with you to your presentation to handle, or that you have waiting for you in your performance area. They can be quite simple, obvious things, or really gimmicky and surprising. What you do will depend on your style. You must be comfortable with what you are doing.

Simple props might include a copy of the newsletter or manual you produced, or examples of paperwork that your listeners will be dealing with.

At a different level, you could make the point that your hardware is out of date by placing a monitor in a dustbin during your presentation. At a yet more advanced level you could carry on a withering branch of a tree to show the ultimate effect of paper wastage.

Few people use these kinds of props in presentations so they are a good way to make sure you are memorable.

Your listeners' imaginations

An often overlooked visual aid is the imagination of your audience. Take the time to describe something to them in detail: so that they can really see the homes, and the children, the dust in the street, the flies, the whole heaving throng of animals, people, cars, and bikes that fight their way along the road every morning, in some countries.

If you do this, prepare your description in advance, have a clear picture in your mind of what you are describing, slow down, and enjoy passing it on to your audience.

Other senses too

4 Choosing and
preparing visual aids

Though not really a *visual* aid, why not involve other senses too? Sounds, smells, and touch could all play a part in a presentation. Imagine trying to convince people that a product is high quality, and handing them the brochure which is on smooth, glossy paper which smells positively luxurious.

Magic moments

If you are doing a business presentation, you might think there is no place in it for magic. But if it suits your style, it's worth considering. You can buy simple card tricks and similar 'magic' at many shops. Imagine making a card disappear and reappear, to emphasize the point that customers are easily lost—and not so easily found again.

Multi-media shows

Once your use of visual aids is confident, you will feel ready to try using more than one at a time. This is very effective, particularly in longer presentations where you need to make more effort to keep the audience's attention.

For example, you could begin by talking and then make some points using the flip chart. Next, it could be PowerPoint, perhaps to summarize some points—and then you could invite some areas for discussion from the audience and write them on the flip chart, and so on.

```
Talk     ──▶  flip chart  ──▶  PowerPoint  ──▶
discuss  ──▶  flip chart  ──▶  summarize
```

To do this you need to be completely relaxed and confident so you need to rehearse everything thoroughly.

57

5 | Using notes

It's definitely faster to prepare notes than to write a full script.

If you are working through this book from start to end, you will have realized by now that some of the preparation you need to do before making a presentation is similar to what you would do for other forms of communication. These include thinking about your audience and aims, devising an appropriate structure, deciding how you will start and finish, and considering how visual aids might help you to put your message across. From now on, the preparation is rather different, because you will be speaking the information, not writing it.

Read, notes, or 'off the cuff'?

The point which often haunts people when they have to present, is knowing they will have to speak for a sustained amount of time in front of a number of people. You have a choice: you could decide to

- talk 'off the cuff'

- read a pre-written script

- talk from notes.

There is a place for all three, as we shall now see. But by far and away the best way to present is to use notes. The secret is in preparing and using those notes well.

Talking 'off the cuff'

Occasionally, you may see a speaker who talks brilliantly for half an hour with no notes or script. The rest of us think: 'I wish I could do that'.

The truth is, some people are born entertainers and will talk about anything at a moment's notice. Often, such speakers are high on entertainment and fluidity, but low on content.

It's also worth noting that most speakers who sail through note-free presentations have spent an enormous amount of time perfecting their act—and that is what it is: an act. If you were to record a polished business speaker, you could find that hardly a word changes from one presentation to the next. That does not down value what they do—but it is not what 'presenting' means to most of us.

No matter how well you know your material, it is always possible to forget what comes next, particularly if you are tired or nervous.

> As I mentioned earlier, there are three reasons for taking this line of action, and the third reason is . . . is . . . is . . .

Also, having notes gives you something do with your hands.

It is also worth considering the impression that can be created in a business environment when speakers arrive with no notes. The audience may think:

- are they going to forget what they are going to say and make this an embarrassing experience for us?

- have they actually bothered preparing for this presentation?

- are they just giving us the same old presentation that they've done so often they know it by heart?

Advice

Only present 'off the cuff' if you are a confident, polished, and thoroughly rehearsed after-dinner speaker. Even then have a note of your host's name and other essential facts!

Recovery tactic

If you forget a point, try involving the audience:

'. . . and the third reason is . . . well, I wonder if *you* can tell *me* what the third reason might be?'

Pre-written scripts

Prepared scripts are deadly, for a number of reasons.

Fact
When reading scripts people tend to
• read too fast
• use a monotone.

1. Readers can't be flexible: they have to read on, no matter how inappropriate the text suddenly appears.

2. The speaker cannot see the audience, to assess how they are reacting.

3. All the audience can see is the top of the speaker's head—plus the occasional glance when they look up.

4. Written language is different from spoken language. It is very hard to write a script which sounds good when it is read aloud.

Those last two sentences are quite straightforward, but even they do not sound quite natural if you read them aloud.

He that hastens, never seems to be master of the situation . . . Pausing properly does more than any other one thing to make one's reading natural and realistic.

Alfred Ayres, *The Essentials of Elocution* (1897)

Try this!

Step 1: Read the two sentences below out loud and consider how they sound.

Written language is different from spoken language. It is very hard to write a script which sounds good when it is read aloud.

Step 2: Now, read the next two sentences aloud, and consider how different they sound.

Written language isn't the same as spoken language. It's really hard to write things down the way you say them.

 Do!

rehearse the script thoroughly so that you can look up every now and then. Even occasional eye contact is better than none.

Even if a script is written appropriately, it is hard to read it well out loud, especially if you are nervous. Readers tend to go far too fast, and they fail to use their voices to help maintain interest in the subject.

When the talk should be scripted

Just occasionally, there is a case for reading pre-prepared texts, though these are not really presentations.

The most common of these is when it's a legal statement. We are all used to seeing people on the TV emerging from court and reading a statement. We also see people in power reading brief explanations of, for example, events such as accidents or company closures. In both instances, they do this because it is essential that the statement is word-for-word as approved by lawyers or others in authority. Presentations are very occasionally read at conferences.

If you have to read aloud, the following guidelines will help.

■ Double space the text.

■ Use a large, clear typeface.

■ Only place a page turn at the end of a paragraph.

■ Indicate the first few words of the next paragraph at the page turns.

■ Read it aloud over and over again, with someone listening and giving feedback if possible.

■ Mark up your reading copy with performance pointers, such as **S L O W L Y**.

■ Rewrite any sentences that sound unnatural.

■ Replace tongue-twisters with easy-to-say words.

■ If people or places have hard-to-pronounce names, write them in your own form of phonetics so that you can say them with ease.

5 Using notes

Working scripts
If you have to read from a script:
● add performance pointers
● mark words and facts to stress
● indicate pauses (P- A- U- S- E)
● use your own phonetics **(fon-ett-icks)**.

See an extract from a working script on page 137

Rewrite tongue-twisters
The poor attendance at this year's matches was the result of being disparaged by a critical cricket critic early in the season.

The poor attendance this year was because the critic who came to our matches early in the season was disparaging.

Notes

Always
have notes, even if
you do not expect to
use them.

The best way to give a presentation is to have notes—or prompts. They keep you on course, help you make sure that you deal with everything you need to cover, and allow you the flexibility to move, add, delete, and generally tailor your information to the audience and to the moment. Notes have none of the disadvantages of off-the-cuff speaking and script reading, and many advantages all their own.

Never
rely on picking up
your notes from a
computer. Too much
can go wrong.

Prompt cards

Many presenters find that the best way to create notes is to write reminders on index cards, rather than sheets of A4 paper. There are many advantages to using cards.

■ They don't shake and tremble if you are nervous.

■ As they are small, they do not create a barrier between the speaker and the audience. This means that you can see the audience, and they can see you.

■ You can hold them in the palm of your hand, and they feel like part of your arm: they do not hamper your gestures and other activities.

Good size
The best cards are
plain white and
measure 6"x 4"
(152 mm x 112 mm).

■ Their size helps remove the temptation to write full sentences, so you can speak naturally from key or prompt words.

■ Writing the cards helps to cement your presentation in your mind because you run through what you will say from each card while you are preparing it.

Waste not
Don't write on the
back of cards.
Instead, use the old
ones for shopping
lists.

■ They are small enough to keep in your pocket—so there's no danger of your presentation papers being lost or moved at the last moment!

Drafting first

Some people draft presentations in full before preparing cards. This can help with thinking the topic through, and uncovers the odd fine phrase to use. However, it is time-consuming and it can be tempting to skip rehearsing and just read the script. Instead, prepare cards straight from your working materials.

How to prepare cards

1. Use the cards in landscape format.

2. Use a strong colour: black or blue, on white.

3. Put a heading on each card.

4. Use large, clear writing which you can read at a glance

5. Write down just as many words as you need to prompt you to remember a point: memory joggers.

The script versus cards

We carried out a survey of the roof to the sports pavilion and hut. The roofs have a very complex structure and have done you good service—they were last replaced 30 years ago. This is a longer period than we would normally expect in this area. However, when we carried out our survey, which was immediately after the spring storms, we found considerable damage.

Background	3

- roof to sports pavilion and hut

- complex structure

- last replaced 30 years ago

- good service – expectations

- survey – January – after storms

Avoid messy cards
If you make a mistake or change your mind, rewrite the card. Messy cards lead to a muddled presentation.

Tip
Highlight the main words by boxing them in a bright colour.

Tip
Make sure you note down:

- names
- numbers
- essential facts
- acronyms in full, in case you are asked (DVD—digital versatile disc)
- memorable phrases you want to use.

Students'
notes
Check the
assessment details
to see if you will have
to hand in your notes
after the
presentation.

Tip
Write performance
pointers in a different
colour so that you're
not tempted to read
them out!

See also Ch. 6,
Rehearsing, and Ch.
7, Giving your
presentation

Tip
Punch holes before
you write your cards,
or you may write
where the hole will
be!

How many cards?

The number of cards you need to use will depend on the presentation you are giving and its content. A single word which reminds you of an anecdote or case history may keep you speaking for several minutes. If another part of your presentation involves facts and statistics which are hard to remember, you will need to use more cards.

Next steps in preparing cards

One of the great advantages of performing from notes on cards is that they are very private: only you need to see them, and they won't be collected in at the end of your presentation to see what you wrote down. Therefore, you can write other points and reminders to yourself:

SMILE   VOICE

You can also make a note of how far into the presentation you should be at any given point. This helps you keep control of the timing, and encourages you onward when you are part way through your presentation.

Finally

1. Number the cards or tie them with a tag—but make sure that, when presenting, you can turn each card over easily.

2. Rehearse.

3. Reduce the number of cards if you can.

4. Rewrite any cards that aren't helping you.

5. Rehearse again.

> ℝecommend that y⟨

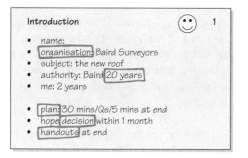

Introduction 😊 1

- name:
- organisation: Baird Surveyors
- subject: the new roof
- authority: Baird 20 years
- me: 2 years

- plan: 30 mins/Qs/5 mins at end
- hope decision within 1 month
- handouts at end

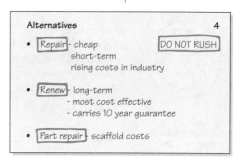

Alternatives 4

- Repair - cheap   DO NOT RUSH
  - short-term
  - rising costs in industry

- Renew - long-term
  - most cost effective
  - carries 10 year guarantee

- Part repair - scaffold costs

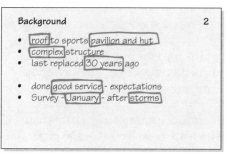

Background 2

- roof to sports pavilion and hut
- complex structure
- last replaced 30 years ago

- done good service - expectations
- Survey - January - after storms

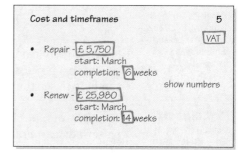

Cost and timeframes 5

VAT

- Repair - £ 5,750
  - start: March
  - completion: 6 weeks
                              show numbers
- Renew - £ 25,980
  - start: March
  - completion: 14 weeks

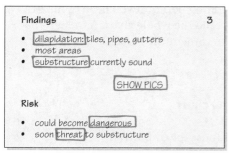

Findings 3

- dilapidation: tiles, pipes, gutters
- most areas
- substructure currently sound

SHOW PICS

Risk

- could become dangerous
- soon threat to substructure

Recommended 6

Renew: can guarantee completion
by summer sports season

Take questions
10 minutes   😊

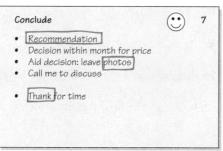

Conclude 😊 7

- Recommendation
- Decision within month for price
- Aid decision: leave photos
- Call me to discuss

- Thank for time

Flow chart style notes

Some presentations are given sitting down and across a desk, rather than standing at the front of the room. This happens in meetings and at college or university where people have to give a presentation as part of a course. If it feels unnatural to have notes on cards in these situations, you might want to try using a flow chart style diagram instead.

Write the flow chart by hand. It's faster than on the PC.

To make any minor changes, just cover the 'mistakes', and photocopy the diagram.

As you can see from the example opposite, with a flow chart you can put the information which might have been on several cards onto a single page. As you do not have to deal with 'page' turns, your across-the-desk presentation then feels less fidgety.

Flow chart style notes are also good for presentations which deal with a process—because there is a 'flow' anyway, and it can help to see the whole picture while you are talking.

Remember!
If seeing the whole picture helps you, it may help your audience as well. Should a version of your notes be a visual aid?

This style of notes is more time-consuming to prepare than pattern diagram notes, which are described over the page. You need to work out the 'flow' before you start writing the notes because you can't keep adding points. If you need to make a big change you may have to redo the whole chart. Although that's a nuisance, it does help to cement the presentation in your mind.

 Do!

rehearse when you plan to use this type of note, to make sure you are comfortable with the format and the prompts you have given yourself.

How to prepare the flow chart

■ Use the paper either landscape or portrait.

■ Use key words: memory joggers.

■ Write in a dark, strong colour.

■ Highlight words with boxing in a bright, clear colour.

■ Make sure you show the 'flow' using arrows.

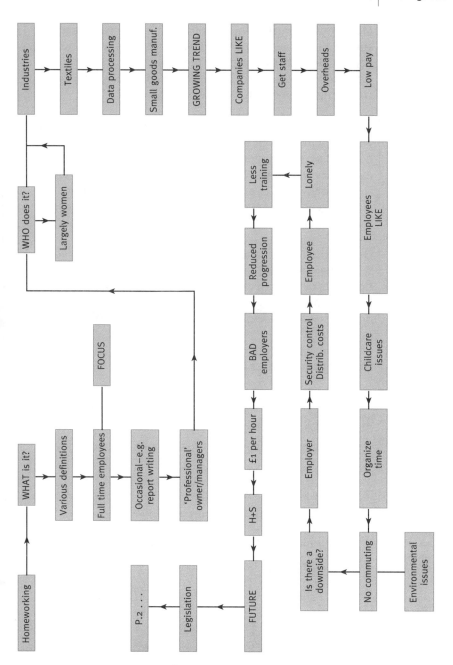

| # Pattern diagrams

See also page 25
for more about
pattern diagrams

Many presenters find they can present from a pattern diagram similar to the one they created when 'brainstorming' ideas. If you decide to do this, you will probably have to redraw the diagram for use as notes as the original is likely to be too confusing and messy to work with.

As you can see from the example opposite, pattern diagrams allow you to put a lot of detail onto one page. But if you go down this route, remember it's essential to know your subject extremely well as you have to work from minimal prompts. Other disadvantages are that they do look rather quirky and eccentric, and they may mean absolutely nothing to anyone, such as your tutor, who may want to see your notes!

Pattern diagrams and flow charts are useful when presenting one-to-one.

On the 'plus' side, pattern diagrams work well for subjects which have a lot of sub-sections, and you maintain some flexibility as you can change the order in which you cover the different areas if you need to. Although you should not need to do this, it can be useful to retain a level of flexibility.

Top tip
Never do anything in a presentation that feels unnatural to you.

How to redraw your pattern diagram

1. Work out your structure before you start.

2. Use the paper in landscape format.

 Do!

find time to rehearse if you plan to use a pattern diagram as notes.
Make sure you can find your way easily from one section to the next. Colours or numbering can help.

3. Begin the diagram toward the top right (at 'one o'clock').

4. Work your way around the clock.

5. Use key words: memory joggers.

6. Write in a dark, strong colour.

7. Highlight essential words with a bright colour.

8. Indicate the flow between sections.

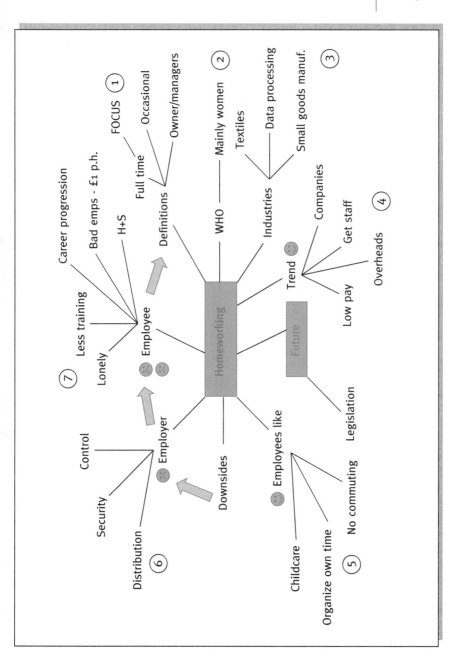

PowerPoint printouts

Speaker's notes

The PowerPoint speaker's notes option prints the slide at the top of an A4 sheet, with a space for your notes below.

Need more help?

To learn in detail about how to create notes or handouts with PowerPoint you will need to do one of the following:
- learn from friends and colleagues
- refer to the manual
- go on a course.

Warning

PowerPoint notes are useful, but A4 sheets may create a barrier and emphasize nervous hands.
Typed notes may be too wordy, and too small to read easily.

Handouts as notes

Another possibility for notes is using what PowerPoint calls handouts. These are intended for audiences who want to take notes. However, they allow you to put several slides onto one sheet, with space alongside for handwriting. Speakers can use the space for their own hand-written notes.

Raising your performance

Extra cards—in colour

You can note additional, optional material on tinted cards which you can spot easily while speaking, even if they are placed part way through your presentation. You can then either use the information or omit it, depending on timing. Typical optional material includes:

■ statistics

■ case histories or examples

■ anecdotes.

Automatic prompt systems

You will have seen conference speakers appearing to address audiences 'off the cuff', by using an automatic prompt system. These work in conjunction with a pre-written script, which is transmitted to monitors placed so that the speaker always has one in view. An operator rolls the text through, following the speaker's speed. The problems associated with reading a script apply.

However, you can also use such prompt systems for your notes. Singers, comics, and other show people do this, finding it an unobtrusive way to be reminded of what comes next.

For major venues and conferences automatic prompt systems are useful: they allow the speaker to appear spontaneous while maintaining eye contact with the audience. However, they are expensive, and most speakers normally only encounter them when their careers have advanced quite a way.

Need more? Or less?
Optional material is useful:
● if an event is running late and you are asked to get it back on time
● if you need to fill in time
● for answering questions.

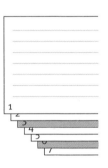

See pages 60–62 for advice on pre-written scripts and notes

Warning
Reading from an automatic prompt is a tricky skill. The supplier is there to help you, and will be the first to advise you that it is essential to rehearse.

6 | Rehearsing

Do I have to?

Rehearsed presentations are always better than those which haven't been rehearsed. The more complex your presentation, and the less experienced you are, the more time you should set aside for rehearsing. If time is short, even one quick run-through will help. But if you can invest time in rehearsing aloud several times, and thoroughly, you will find it a transforming experience.

Find out what changes you need to make

When you rehearse you will discover the changes you need to make. You may realize that parts of the presentation are dull, or too complex. You may decide to add a visual, or experiment with some of the 'Raising your performance' tricks in this and other chapters of this book.

You will also discover where to add weight and significance to sections of your presentation or to individual words within sentences, which you can then mark on your notes.

> We should think about—and I really **do** mean **think** about—making these changes before the end of the year.

Always
find time to rehearse, especially if
• you are using visual aids for the first time
• you are using technology
• you are presenting as a team.

 Do!
try to leave a day between your final rehearsal and performance to avoid the 'Have I already said this?' syndrome.

Start conquering nerves

If you rehearse you will feel less nervous on the day. Your brain will be telling you that you have done this—and survived!—before. It will start to convince you that perhaps you should not feel so nervous about presenting after all. (Your brain *will* be saying this—even if you can't hear it!)

Get used to your notes and visual aids

While rehearsing you will get used to handling your notes, and your visual aids. In both cases, you may discover that you need to add to them, or delete from them. In particular, you have a chance to make sure that your prompt words and performance pointers work effectively.

If you do rehearse thoroughly, you are more likely to be able to relax and create the impression that you are speaking spontaneously.

Check the timing

A rehearsal is the only way to check the timing of your presentation. You should obviously check your watch at the start and end of the rehearsal. You might want to check how long you should take to other certain key moments, such as when you move on to a different area.

If you don't rehearse, all the rest of your preparation work may be wasted.

Most speakers go slightly faster on the day.

If you are using PowerPoint, you can set the system to record the time you have each slide visible during your rehearsal. It will remember the timings, and change slides automatically during your performance. It sounds an interesting idea, but the computer will expect your timing to be *exactly* the same as at rehearsal. If you happen to go faster or slower than you did during rehearsal, you and your slides will not be synchronized. If you are less than confident about presenting, it may be distracting—something extra to worry about, rather than a help.

How many rehearsals?

✗ Don't!

over-rehearse. If you do too many rehearsals you may lose the sharpness you need on the day.

Three rehearsals seems to be the ideal number for many people. This allows you to make each rehearsal more detailed and closer to what you will do on 'the day'. But the number of rehearsals will depend on the complexity of what you plan to do, and your level of experience.

At the most **basic level**, you would run through your presentation in private—but out loud—imagining yourself using your visual aids. This allows you to concentrate on the content of your presentation.

Seeking feedback

If you are inviting comments on your presentation, choose people you trust to be honest.

Ask them what they like about your presentation, and what you might need to improve.

Ask for comments on:
- what they thought of the content
- how your presentation style comes across
- how useful your visual aids are.

At an **intermediate level**, you would give your presentation in front of others, seeking their feedback and comments. You would use your visual aids at this stage, so that you get used to handling them.

At the most **advanced level**, you would go through your presentation at the venue, or at a simulated venue, again with an audience who will give you feedback.

When time is short

If there isn't time for several rehearsals, compromise and choose the intermediate level described above. As a minimum:

- work your way carefully through your notes 'hearing' the presentation in your head;

- time yourself;

- practise using your visual aids, so that you can set the venue the way you want it;

- put special effort into the beginning and the end.

See page 134 for advice on how to prepare a presentation in a hurry

How to rehearse

Whether you decide to do just one rehearsal or all three, there are some pointers you should definitely follow.

■ Rehearse out loud—you need to hear your voice, and to find those impossible-to-pronounce tongue-twisters.

■ Always rehearse in a quiet room. Do not have the radio, TV, or CD player on the go while you are rehearsing. You need to hear your voice.

■ Always use the notes you plan to use on the day.

■ Rehearse on your feet, sitting down, or mixing the two if that's what you plan to do on the day.

■ Always rehearse with your actual visual aids—not substitutes.

■ Take it seriously—you need to get the adrenalin working.

■ You may feel foolish when you start rehearsing and could well have a false start. Don't let that worry you—it's just a result of feeling silly because you are talking to yourself!

■ If you are rehearsing alone, don't bother with a video camera. They are useful on training courses because the operator will follow you, and will use close-up and distance shots.

■ Don't bother with recorders. Most of us dislike the sound of our recorded voices—only the best machines capture the true nature of a voice. The real person is more than a disembodied voice anyway.

■ There's no real benefit to presenting to a mirror as you have to stand in the same spot all the time, and they invite the speaker to 'pose'.

■ Amend and improve your notes after each rehearsal.

Practise essential tongue-twisters

Our next winner is Bagshot's Peggy Babcock.

Next, we added the pentaerythritol to the poly(ethyleneglycol terephthalate).

We have a hold-up in the aluminiuming process.

This is a purely phenomenological argument.

See pages 102–3 on how to rehearse as a team

 Do!

amend your notes and visual aids after each rehearsal.

Raising your performance

At all levels

- Write intermediate timings on notes and check your progress against the clock.

> Half-way—10.30

- Invite formal audience feedback from your rehearsal audience by giving them a sheet of things to look for.

- Push your comfort boundaries by experimenting with the unfamiliar. Try using a different kind of visual aid, or walking right round the room while you are speaking, or using a dramatic gesture. You can always decide against doing these things later.

At the basic level

- Use every chance to practise using your voice. Enjoy saying your presentation aloud
  - in the shower
  - walking the dog
  - in the car.

- If possible, rehearse in a room that is about the size and shape of the one you expect to present in. At colleges and in the workplace it's often possible to borrow a room for a couple of hours.

- Learn the opening and close of your presentation by heart, so that you can really concentrate on the audience at these important moments.

At the intermediate level

- Invite non-experts to your rehearsal. They will be likely to concentrate more on performance than content, but will also be able to tell you how clear the content is, and where a visual aid would have helped them to understand.

- Invite your audience to role-play. They could be grumpy adolescents, retired people, or anxious staff. Preparing yourself to present to people who are having a specific kind of reaction to what you are saying can increase your ability to cope with bored or worried-looking people on the day.

Try this
Practise finding a specific visual aid or point in your notes, in case your audience asks you to return to a particular point.

- Invite your role-play audience to ask questions or make statements in character! This can be a lot of fun, and helps you to deal with tricky questions if they arise.

> Can you just explain what existentialism actually means, please?
>
> I think there's a mistake in the second column of figures!
>
> What-ya doin' after school, miss?

At the advanced level

- Lay out chairs around the room, making sure you put some right at the back of the room, and one on your extreme left and right.

See Ch. 10, Managing your presentation, for room layouts

- Put something striking on some of the chairs—a pile of books, a bunch of flowers, a teddy bear. Then, notice how often you see these things during your presentation.

See Ch. 7, Giving your presentation, for advice on pausing

- Practise using long pauses, for dramatic effect.

7 | Giving your presentation

The purpose of all the planning, structuring, and rehearsing which you do before your presentation is to allow you to appear to be speaking to your audience spontaneously. But often we find that, despite all our efforts, as the presentation approaches we feel somewhere between anxious and petrified. So before going any further, let's deal with the all-consuming issue of what we'll call 'nerves'.

Why do we get nervous?

The fear of looking foolish

It is said that presenting—that any kind of public speaking—is one of the greatest dreads people have. Even confident and experienced speakers say they are sometimes nervous. When you analyse it, the fear normally comes down to just one point: we are afraid of looking foolish. So we worry about:

Remember
The unpleasant sensations which many people speak of experiencing when they are doing a presentation are a perfectly normal, physical reaction to being in an unfamiliar and unknown situation.

- what we should say;

- forgetting what we want to say;

- people not listening to us;

- being looked at by people;

- being given a hard time by people;

- being asked awkward questions that we cannot answer.

Because these thoughts make us nervous, we also worry about other points:

- Who should we look at?

- How should we stand?

- What should we do with our hands?

- Will people be able to hear us?

> *Visualize*
> Build a positive picture of yourself doing your presentation, looking and sounding the way you would like.

If we are using visual aids, we will add a lot more worries:

- Suppose we can't manage them?

- Suppose the technology lets us down?

- What if everything goes wrong, and I end up looking foolish?

In this way, we argue ourselves round in a circle and end up feeling worse and worse about the idea of presenting.

Our instincts say 'Don't!'

As children we are often reprimanded for 'showing off', 'drawing attention to ourselves', or 'wanting to be the centre of attention'. So we associate being the centre of attention with being 'wrong' or 'naughty'! Then, when we are adults, people invite us to give a presentation—to be the centre of attention! No wonder we feel nervous—our upbringing has probably convinced us that this is something we should definitely not be doing.

> *There is nothing either good or bad, but thinking makes it so.*
> William Shakespeare, *Hamlet*, Act 2, Sc. 2, line 259 (1601)

The situation is important

We also get nervous because there is often a lot riding on our success: it might mean winning a new client, getting that great job, or prising a few extra marks out of the examiner.

What happens when we are nervous?

People are often nervous about presenting. We have looked at why that might be the case. It can also be helpful to know what happens to our bodies when we get nervous, and why.

When we are nervous or scared, our bodies switch on their 'flight or fight' mechanism, and pump out extra adrenalin. This is the hormone which allows us to cope with difficult situations, such as danger: it prepares our bodies to run away or to fight by causing physical changes.

■ The heart pumps fast and hard to help us run away.

■ Blood pumps to our legs so that we can run to safety.

■ We tense our muscles ready to run away or fight.

Of course, when we are presenting we are neither fighting nor running away (as much as we might want to!) so the effects of the adrenalin can get in the way. We become aware of a number of unpleasant adrenalin-prompted sensations.

■ Our hands and face get hot, red, and sweaty.

■ Our legs wobble.

■ We keep popping to the toilet.

■ We struggle to reach the end of sentences.

■ Our hands tremble.

■ Our breathing becomes shallow.

■ Our voice doesn't behave and our mouth goes dry.

■ We have a feeling of 'butterflies in the stomach'.

Experience says
A nervous presenter was once heard to comment: 'Whenever I have to give a presentation, all my saliva rushes to the palms of my hands!'

Tip
Sweaty hands? While waiting to present sit with your hands palms up. This makes it harder to clench your fists, and lets the air get to your palms. It also helps you to relax your shoulders, which in turn helps prevent a 'strangled' voice.

Adrenalin is good for presenters!

The good news is that adrenalin also really helps you to do an excellent presentation. Many actors speak of being hopelessly and wretchedly nervous when waiting to go on stage. Both they and people who do presentations regularly say that when you don't feel nervous before you start, then it is time to start worrying about your performance!

Don't panic!
There's good news about these side-effects of nerves:
- audiences are usually unaware of them
- they can be controlled
- they can be disguised.

This is because all that adrenalin-fed energy can be pumped into what you are doing. Redirected, it can keep you alert and fuel the enthusiasm and commitment that you want to show your listeners.

Because adrenalin is there to help you cope in an emergency, it enables you to cope in the unlikely event of something going wrong. Adrenalin is what allows you to find the perfect answer to a tricky question, or to make light of the fact that one of your graphs is upside down. Well-handled, such mishaps will be overlooked and forgotten by the audience.

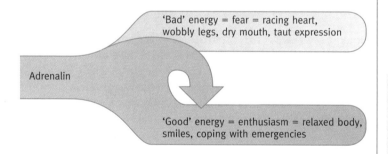

Adrenalin

'Bad' energy = fear = racing heart, wobbly legs, dry mouth, taut expression

'Good' energy = enthusiasm = relaxed body, smiles, coping with emergencies

Shock! Surprise!
Former British Prime Minister Margaret Thatcher said: 'I am nervous every time I get up to make a major speech. I am nervous every time I go into the House of Commons.'

How to channel adrenalin

To channel your adrenalin, do not think about yourself. Instead, concentrate on:

■ your audience

■ the message you are putting across to them.

How we form impressions of people

Research shows that we make up our minds about people in just a few minutes, based on:

- how they look—professional and in control, or tense;
- how they sound—lively and enthusiastic, or bored;
- what they say—the actual content of what they say.

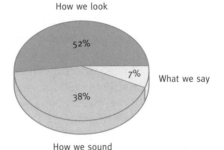

How we look

52%

7% What we say

38%

How we sound

Look good

We make up our minds how we are going to react to someone before they speak. So, if you look and sound confident, people are more likely to decide it's a good presentation.

Be a swan

Think how calm a swan looks as it drifts along the river. That's how you should aim to look. But remember that while the swan looks serene, it is paddling away under the surface.

Content matters

Although we create strong impressions of people based on the way they seem it's no good being a confident and fun presenter who talks rubbish.

Try this!

Imagine someone has written a novel which has become an immediate best-seller. You have never seen the author and know nothing about the book. Then, there's the author on TV—*but you have the sound turned down*. You are likely to decide what you think of the author quite quickly. You think they look fun, intelligent, shifty, or conventional. You may decide you'd like their novel.

Now, imagine turning the sound up—but *finding they are speaking in a foreign language*. They may sound just as you expected, or completely different—but your *expectation* has been based entirely on how the person *looks*. Now you will add to your impression the way they *sound*: perhaps enthusiastic, fluent, desperate or boring. But you are still not basing your opinion on what they *say*—they are speaking a foreign language.

As presenters, one of our challenges is to make sure that we look right—that our 'body language' is positive—so that people have confidence in what we are saying.

The 'magic circle'

We have seen that adrenalin is good for you—if you channel it correctly—and that we form impressions of each other based on the way we look and seem. There's another fact to bear in mind that will reduce nerves: you can make your body believe you are relaxed.

Don't!

focus on the things that can go wrong. It's bound to make you feel nervous.

Smiles produce endorphins—'feel good' hormones. If you smile, your subconscious will think 'I'm smiling—I must be relaxed', and will tell your body to feel and look confident. Your audience will see how confident you are and become engaged and interested. Seeing this will help you to smile, so your subconscious will think 'I must be relaxed'—and round this 'magic circle' you go!

Do!

plan, to make sure you give a successful presentation. Imagine how well you are going to do it, then you will do well.

Smile

"I must be relaxed"

You feel relaxed

You look relaxed

You get good 'vibes'

When a situation makes smiling inappropriate you should still avoid looking too severe, with a clenched jaw and a frown. Have a neutral expression—kind but serious.

Serious matters

Avoid big smiles when it's bad news such as
- redundancies
- accidents
- bad results.

Try this!

Stand facing a full-length mirror and think about something that makes you really angry, or that you feel resentful about. Look at the expression on your face. Notice your eyes, the position of your jaw, your posture, and your breathing.

Now, think about something that makes your happy, or an experience that you really enjoyed, and note the changes. They will be subtle, but they will be there.

Consider which of these presenters you would prefer to see.

Smile!

Smiling will help you to breathe naturally, and you will be less likely to experience the negative effects of adrenalin.

Body language

The statistics which show that people assess speakers in part by their appearance have little to do with how handsome or beautiful they are! The audience's opinions are formed subconsciously by factors which speakers can control—their expression, how they stand, sit, move, their eye contact, and their clothes.

Let your posture help you present

One of the most important aspects of your presentation will be the way you stand, because:

- people who stand well look confident;

- when you look confident, your body tricks you into thinking that you are confident;

- if you stand well, you can breathe more fully, which helps you to project your voice, and to feel calm.

He gave me his hand; which I didn't know what to do with, as it did nothing for itself.

Charles Dickens, *David Copperfield*

Good news
If you start by making the audience feel confident in you, you are on your way to presenting well.

If you look calm and professional, people will believe you are!

> **Try this!**
>
> Stand and face a mirror as if you are really bored and feeling negative—perhaps your train is late and you have been on the platform for ten minutes, only to hear there's a another twenty minutes to wait. Notice your body position.
>
> Now, stand as if you feel very happy and confident about something. Perhaps you have just got an excellent mark for a piece of work, or a pat on the back from your boss. Again, notice your body position.

The point of this experiment is not how you stood in each case—but that you knew what to do. If we all know what bored and negative looks like, and what happy and confident looks like, so does our audience. They will 'read' how we are feeling.

Aim for a natural and relaxed-looking position. Some people stand so rigidly when they present that they look like soldiers on duty. Others stoop over their notes which makes them look insecure—and they talk to the floor! Stand upright and firm, but not stiffly, which will make you look tense and can 'strangle' the voice.

You are aiming to have your body in alignment, with your spine in a long, soft S curve. Your head should be up and back, with your chin tucked in and your shoulders relaxed and down.

Wrong posture— wrong voice
Your posture affects your voice, including how audible it is.

Try this!

Stand in front of a full-length mirror as naturally as possible. Look at yourself both face-on and sideways. Then imagine a piece of string attached to the crown of your head, gently pulling you up straight. Let your shoulders hang loosely.

Many speakers find the most comfortable standing position is with the feet about hip width apart and one foot slightly in front of the other.

It's good to move about during your presentation. If the room or the audience is large, movement helps you to 'reach' more people. You can get close to them, or even walk right round the room if it serves your purpose and suits your style.

It is easier to do this if you think of having a 'base' position—a point to which you return and from which you can move, by taking a few, definite steps and then stopping

Make your movements definite. Do not 'rock', sway, or dance on the spot. People seem to do this when they think they must stand in one place throughout their presentation, though their instinct is to move about.

All these movements are wasted energy, so if you're tempted to fidget, *move* and divert the energy into your presentation.

Tip
To find the correct position for your head, imagine holding a grapefruit under your chin with one hand. If you imagine holding an apple, your head will be dropped too far down, and if you imagine a melon it will be too far back!

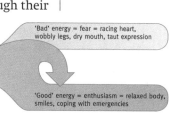

See page 81 for the effects of adrenalin on body language

'Bad' energy = fear = racing heart, wobbly legs, dry mouth, taut expression

Adrenalin

'Good' energy = enthusiasm = relaxed body, smiles, coping with emergencies

If you are presenting one-to-one, or to just a couple of people, consider whether it would be more appropriate to sit for the presentation.

Suit the action to the word, the word to the action.

William Shakespeare, *Hamlet*, Act 3, Sc. 2, line 19 (1601)

Did you know?

Gestures are a minefield when presenting overseas. For example, the 'thumbs up' sign usually means 'good', but in some countries it is extremely rude.

If in doubt, check with the Embassy before presenting overseas.

See page 140 for a book with lots of information about gestures and their meaning

Stand, rather than sit

If you can choose, present standing up—you will have more authority as people will be literally 'looking up to you'. Also, when standing you can breathe and project your voice more clearly, and make better eye contact with your audience.

However, many presentations are given sitting down. If you have to do this, all the above points about body language count—and there are a few additional points to think about.

Take particular care to make eye contact with the people sitting to your extreme right and left. They are 'danger zones' where people often get missed out.

You still need to watch your posture so sit tall in the chair.

Use hands and gestures for emphasis

Hands contribute enormously to communication, so if you keep them in one position it's a missed opportunity, and it looks dull.

If you can forget about your hands they will behave naturally and all sorts of gestures will appear. You may touch your heart to show feeling, or use wide, open arm movements to express welcome or enthusiasm.

For less formal presentations, it's usually acceptable to put one hand in your jacket or trouser pocket for part of your presentation. This can look very relaxed and confident—but remove keys and small change so that you don't 'jangle'.

Gesturing is not the same as fidgeting. Gestures are definite movements used for emphasis. Fidgeting is repeated, unconscious action—such as finger tapping or playing with a flip chart pen. Fidgeting makes you look nervous and is distracting—so don't do it!

Use your face to show feelings

We are intuitive about faces and 'read' their expressions. We spot and interpret even minute traces of smiles or scowls. The more you use your face, the more you reinforce what you are saying.

Make eye contact

When people lie, are shifty or untrustworthy they often don't make eye contact. Your audience is more likely to trust and believe you if you look at them. Also, by looking at people, you can tell if they are confused or uninspired by what you are saying, or whether they are entertained and enthusiastic.

Eye-eye!
Eye contact means eye ball to eye ball, not somewhere around someone's forehead, or over their shoulder.

Avoid looking at any one person for too long as they may feel they are being stared at. Look at each person for three to five seconds. If you are answering someone's question, you can maintain eye contact with them throughout a *short* reply.

Avoid looking at one person, then their neighbour, and then the next and so on around the room. Aim to move your focus from one part of the group to another, moving your eyes steadily. If you move your eyes too fast you can look shifty.

A large room?

If the room is really large, think of it as a giant M and look at people at different points of the letter, for example go from the bottom left to the top right, to the middle and so on. The audience will think you are looking at everyone in the room.

$$3 \quad 2$$
$$\mathsf{M}$$
$$1 \quad 5 \quad 4$$

Spectacles?

If you wear spectacles for presenting, make sure that people to your extreme right and left know that you are making eye contact with them by turning your head very slightly in their direction when you look at them.

Let your smile work with you

You really will feel better and people really will think you are relaxed and confident if you smile. But your smile should be a natural one—not a big cheesy grin—and you shouldn't switch it on and off, like a light bulb.

Sometimes a smile may not be appropriate, for example in presentations about accidents or bad results. This does not mean that you have to have a fixed and glum face. Let your face be lively and expressive, and let it reflect what you are saying. A more serious expression for serious points, a slight smile for lighter points.

If a smile is not appropriate, simply relax your facial muscles, especially the 'hinge' of your jaw (without gaping!). A clenched jaw will make your saliva dry up. Remember, you can always smile when greeting your audience—just not too much if the topic is serious.

You still need to vary your expression when talking one-to-one. Avoid 'frozen face' syndrome.

Dress the part

It's traditional for the presenter to dress slightly more formally than the audience to set their separateness and authority. If the presentation is at the level of the tailored suit or dinner jackets, the speaker is dressed the same as the audience.

If your audience is in shirtsleeves, you might want to keep your jacket on. For audiences wearing jeans and T-shirts, you might choose trousers or jeans and jacket. If you are presenting on 'safety' to swim-suited tourists, you might want to wear shorts.

Presentations are not the time for new clothes. You need to have made sure that your clothes don't ride up, fall down, crease, or make you sweaty *before* the presentation. You have enough to think about without worrying about what you are wearing.

Hairy facts!
People need to see your face so fringes should leave your eyes visible. Tie back long hair—playing with stray locks will make you look insecure.

Any style or colour goes—but if your presentation is to sell new software to civil servants, will a green Mohican really help?

Projecting your personality

Don't try to be 'someone else' when you are presenting. You are not an actor, so don't try to be formal if you are normally friendly, or 'one of the lads' if you are usually a distant manager. You should be yourself, which can be hard when you are nervous. You can achieve it in part by concentrating on the audience and what you want to achieve.

> **Tip**
> Project your voice and personality to the corners of the room. Fill your space and people will want to listen to you.

Try this!

Imagine you have been outside the place where you work, study, or hold meetings, and have seen there's a building on fire, nearby but some distance from where you are. When you get back you would probably announce 'There's a building on fire along the road.' Hold in your mind the image of how you would do that.

Next, imagine that it's the building that you are in that's on fire. You would say something like 'Get out! The building's on fire!'

How would you look, sound, and move in this second situation, compared to the first?

> *. . . how I long for a little ordinary human enthusiasm. Just enthusiasm —that's all.*
>
> John Osborne *Look Back in Anger*, Act 1 (1956)

In the second situation, you would almost certainly be louder. You would be experiencing a kind of **excitement**, so you would use bolder gestures. You would inject **energy** into what you say to make sure your message reaches right round the room and is heard by as many people as possible. You would certainly have **enthusiasm** for making sure your message was received and understood. These three important qualities will help you to project your personality.

Use the three Es when presenting one-to-one or to small groups—just use less than you would use for a larger group.

Remember, you are presenting, not chatting.

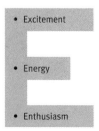

- Excitement
- Energy
- Enthusiasm

Present with 'Ease'

Add the three Es at the right level for your audience and subject.

Be (and look) confident

See Ch. 6, Rehearsing

It's hard for even the most bubbly personality to 'escape' from someone who looks nervous. It's definitely easier to project your personality if you feel confident about your subject and the presentation you are giving. If you are following the advice in this book, you should have a well thought out and planned talk, with good visual aids. If you feel nervous, despite all your preparation, there are still things you can do to help reduce your nerves.

Smile
Never forget, smiles produce endorphins —the 'feel good' hormones.

Concentrate on your audience

Keep breathing
Breath is the energy which relaxes your nerves and fuels your presentation.

There are a number of 'places' a presenter *could* focus their attention when presenting. You *could* focus on yourself, your audience, or the presentation.

Speakers who focus on themselves almost always fail to project their personalities. They are also the ones who seem to feel most nervous because they think about how they are feeling, and not what they are trying to achieve.

The best presentations are the ones where the speaker has prepared and rehearsed so well that they are confident about every aspect of the presentation. That allows them to divide their concentration between the audience and the presentation—and they keep most of their focus and concentration on the audience.

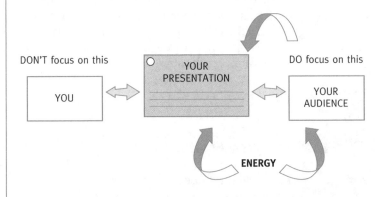

DON'T focus on this

YOU

YOUR PRESENTATION

DO focus on this

YOUR AUDIENCE

ENERGY

Practise visualization and 'cementing'

Two more techniques for controlling nerves involve using your imagination. What you need to do is described below. You may need to read through the techniques a couple of times so that you can go smoothly through the whole process.

Visualization

Close your eyes, and visualize yourself giving an outstanding presentation. See how you are standing, feel yourself breathing slowly and calmly, watch yourself handling your visual aids. Then, hear yourself: what you are saying, how your voice sounds. Hear yourself pause, and watch as you move about the performance area. Really concentrate on the sounds and image, and pause on the image for about half a minute. Recall that image as you begin your presentation.

Cementing

Remember a time when you felt really relaxed, perhaps on a beach or in a garden, or walking in the country. Recall how you felt, and looked. Put yourself in the picture and then make the image really big: intensify the sounds and colours, feel how calm and contented you were. Then, snap your fingers. The sound and action of the 'snap' will cement the relaxed feel in your mind. If you snap your fingers just before you present, the sound and action will revert you to that relaxed time. This technique is so effective that it really is worth practising until it works for you.

Breathe

Deep breathing is the route to feeling calm which many professional performers favour. There's more about breathing and breath control later in the chapter, when we deal with making the most of your voice.

Breathing

Try this simple breathing exercise to relax.

- Breathe in through your nose to a count of ten seconds
- Breathe out though your mouth to a count of ten seconds
- Repeat two or three times—no more.

See further reading and resources in Part B

Sounding good

Singing in the rain?

If you live alone, the first time you speak on the day of your presentation could be when you address the audience!·

Warm up your voice by singing in the shower, or speaking to people on the train, on the bus—or talk to yourself (before you leave home!).

Most people have been to a lecture or presentation where the speaker mumbles and is hard to hear, or who has had a dull voice. And most of us have found that, when this happens, it can be hard to concentrate on what is being said.

So, the two areas which are essential to consider when it comes to the way you sound during your presentation are:

■ how to make sure you are audible;

■ how to make sure you sound interesting.

The equipment

We all have more-or-less the same vocal equipment, which in simplified terms is made up of:

■ a set of vocal cords;

■ breathing apparatus in the form of lungs and diaphragm;

■ a collection of tubes and cavities (such as sinuses and nasal passages);

■ a collection of muscles (lips, tongue, and almost a hundred tiny facial ones);

■ other pieces of anatomy, including teeth, and hard and soft palate (the areas of the roof of your mouth, behind your upper teeth).

The difference between an audible and interesting speaker and a mumbling dull one lies in the way we use this basic equipment.

Being audible

In everyday speech we only use a small part of the capacity of our vocal equipment. We don't breathe deeply and we don't exercise all the muscles which allow us to project the voice. When we have to present—particularly if we have to speak for 15 or 20 minutes—we are doing the verbal equivalent of running a marathon. As we all know, you can't run a marathon without training—and you have to warm up before you start. Similarly, for presentations, you need to 'train' your voice and 'warm up' before you start to speak.

There are three things you must do to make sure you are audible to your audience.

■ Breathe deeply to fuel your voice with breath.

■ Let the sound escape by not trying to speak to a room full of people while hardly moving your mouth.

■ Pronounce each word clearly and fully.

How to breathe *properly*!

Air is the fuel which allows you to keep going, and to project your voice without it strangling or squeaking. Unfortunately, most of the time we only partially fill our lungs—especially if we are nervous.

When you breathe deeply and fully, you take your breath in to a spot really low in your ribcage. Just raising your shoulders, which is what many people do when asked to 'take a deep breath', isn't the right thing to do. Instead, when you breathe in you should be able to feel your ribs move outward—that is, sideways, not upwards. You can feel this right round your body and on your spine. While your ribs go outward, your diaphragm goes downward. The combination of these two movements makes the biggest possible space to be filled with air.

Tip
Never think you haven't got 'time' to take a deep breath during a presentation. To your audience, it will seem like just a momentary pause.

Extra benefits
Deep breathing is one of the most effective ways of reducing nerves—and the one generally favoured by professional performers.

Try this!

To feel what a really deep breath feels like, stand up straight and relaxed, and place your hands at the bottom of your ribs, with your finger-tips touching. Now, keeping your shoulders down and relaxed, take a deep breath sending it so far down that it forces your finger-tips slightly apart.

Then, move your hands round to your back and place them either side of your spine. Again, keep your shoulders down and see whether you can breathe inward and make your hands move outwards.

You may need several goes to get the feeling. When you do— that's what a deep breath is, and that's the part of your body you should breathe from when you are presenting.

When you have the knack of breathing deeply, learn to control the outward flow by adding an audible sigh, or blowing the air out slowly through your mouth to a count of ten seconds and build up the count with time.

Open wide!

It's no use taking breaths that would fuel an opera singer through a long aria, if there's no chance for the sound to escape. You need to open your mouth wide, and move your lips, for the sound to reach your audience. This doesn't mean gaping and making yourself look silly—simply proving to people that you are a presenter, not a ventriloquist.

Something else to try

Moving your mouth as little as possible, say 'extraordinary bubbles bouncing on the marmalade'. Then say it moving your mouth as much as possible, then moving it naturally. Hear how differently your voice 'travels' with scarcely any extra effort from you.

Articulate the words

Now you've created the sound (by breathing) and have found out how to let the sound escape (by opening your mouth), you need to make sure the sound is clear.

We all speak differently and, thank goodness, it is no longer considered odd to have a regional accent. What matters is being heard and understood. English speakers often slur over some of the syllables in words. They might say 'sillbulls' instead of syll-a-bles, 'diffrence' instead of diff-er-ence, or 'particly' instead of part-tic-u-lar-ly. When we listen to speakers who do that, we have to listen hard, which means that we concentrate more on listening and less on understanding.

To help yourself articulate the words, really hear what you are saying and pronounce each word fully and clearly. (Oddly, we tend to do this anyway when we are talking to people from overseas, or when we are on mobile phones!)

These exercises will give some of your speaking 'bits' a workout:

- Chew an imaginary, but large, gooey toffee for several minutes to work your mouth and facial muscles.

- Blow raspberries to relax your lips.

- Hum a tune to get your vocal resonators working.

Vocal exercises will get more speaking muscles working.

Freddy's teddy's name is Eddy.
She opened a slop shop in Wapping.
Mr Knightly's likely to be slightly sprightly nightly.
The lunar module leaves for the moon at noon.
Betty's beautiful border's blossoming blue begonias.

Read out loud

Practise using your voice well by reading aloud. In private is fine, but reading to children who want you to 'do all the voices' is excellent presentation practice.

Listen and learn!

Listen to news broadcasters on TV. They use a wide range of notes.

The great source of pleasure is variety. Uniformity must tire at last, though it be uniformity of excellence.

Samuel Johnson, *Lives of the English Poets* (1779/81)

Sound interesting

When hypnotists put people into a trance they speak softly and drop their voices at the end of sentences. Many presenters do the same—and risk sending the audience to sleep! Instead you need to vary the sound of your voice.

In everyday speech most of us use only a small number of the very many notes our voices can reach. Without using silly, funny voices we can gently move our voices up high and down low. Presenters who do this are often described as 'being interesting' when really it's the voice that is interesting. If you can get the knack of using more notes in your voice during your presentation than you do normally, you too will sound interesting.

Try this!

Try saying 'extraordinary bubbles bouncing on the marmalade' hitting syllables as high and low as you can.

Go on—have fun, and really 'play' with your voice.

Colour your voice

Another way to sound interesting, and to help your audience to stay listening, is to colour your voice. This means using it to express different moods. Here is something else for you to experiment with.

Try this!

Below is a very simple, every day sentence. See whether you can say it in a way that implies a lot more than its simple meaning. Try sounding angry, bored, seductive, amused, doubtful, impatient, and so on. Discover what your voice is capable of!

I think it is going to rain this afternoon.

Avoid dropping your voice

Avoid dropping your voice at the end of each sentence, to stop your audience dozing off.

For example, on the above sentence, the normal 'tune' of the sentence is to drop your voice on 'off' to the extent that it might be almost inaudible. As a presenter you need to give the word 'off' an equal push to the rest of the sentence. This does not mean raising your voice at the sentence end—that makes statements sound like questions and can make you seem uncertain. Just keep the momentum going by landing on the final word with some force—as if more words followed.

Note
Putting force on the final word of a sentence will sound odd to you. So long as it is not exaggerated, it will sound fine to your audience. Listen to newscasters to hear what they sound like.

Try this!

Say these two sentences.

I would now like to make a start on my presentation.

I would now like to make a start on my presentation to you.

Do you give 'presentation' more 'push' in the second sentence?

Count on pauses
Nervous about pausing? Count the seconds off in your head: 'one . . . two . . . three . . .' and then continue.

Add variety, add pleasure

As well as being audible, clear, musical, and keeping the momentum of your voice going right to the end of each sentence, you need to sound interesting by adding variety to your voice.

■ Vary the pace: speak quickly, speak slowly. Speed up or slow down gradually, or quickly.

■ Vary the volume: speak loudly, speak more softly. Get gradually louder or softer, or change the volume suddenly.

■ Never under-estimate the value of a pause, particularly mid-sentence.

When I looked at our results for the last year I realized that . . . this team has out-performed all our expectations.

The notes I handle no better than many pianists. But the pauses between the notes—ah, that is where the art resides!

Pianist Artur Schnabel, *Chicago Daily News* (1958)

8 | Team presentations

Why teams present

Students at college or university sometimes have to give a team presentation to develop their team-working skills, and to allow longer presentations on a single subject, so that the topic is covered in more depth. Participants on training courses also have to report back on group projects by means of a presentation. Here, there is an element of competition, with each team wanting to 'win'.

People in the workplace also give team presentations. Here, team members could know each other, such as when an information technology group gives a presentation about a new system. When this happens, each hardware or software specialist speaks about their own area.

Other workplace teams are created when companies are going all-out to win a contract. They create a team from different parts of the organization to show a range of skills. A marketing consultancy may need to show that they have writers, designers, event organizers, and public relations specialists.

When presenting as a team you need to:

■ add in a pre-planning stage;

■ approach the preparation slightly differently;

■ cover extra points during the rehearsals;

■ think about additional things on the day.

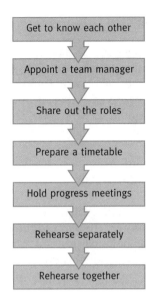

Pre-planning for success

Your pre-planning can probably be covered in a single meeting. It will help the rest of your preparation to go smoothly, and save you time because you will work well together and avoid overlaps and gaps.

Get to know each other

As a presentation team you have to work together closely to ensure that the end result is all you want it to be. There could be disruptions and disagreements along the way, and these will be easier to deal with if you get to know each other first. This is particularly important for teams which have been brought together specifically for the presentation, but can also be true when you seem to know each other quite well already. Presentations can bring out unexpected qualities in people—both good and bad.

Getting to know you
Get to know your team members by
- organizing a fundraising event
- doing a quiz night
- having a social evening
- holding a sports event
- playing games
- doing quick-fire, one-minute presentations.

Appoint a team manager

This may not be the person who has been responsible for a project, the most senior person, or the 'brightest' person on a course. It should be the person who is most likely to be able to manage the whole process of preparing and giving the presentation. They should be persuasive, tactful, strong, have good 'people' skills, and be excellent time managers.

Appoint a team administrator

For larger presentations, particularly competitive business presentations, you may need a team administrator. The administrator would book meeting and rehearsal rooms, do the team's photocopying, and possibly create the visual aids.

Share out the team roles

Quite apart from the content of the presentation, there are a number of roles that need to be carried out in the team to keep it working well together. Distribute roles on the basis of personal strengths. If someone is particularly good with technology, another artistic, one a naturally fluent speaker, and one a natural manager, make use of those strengths.

If your team doesn't have a spread of skills and abilities, give the roles to those with most enthusiasm for the tasks.

Prepare a timetable

Agree a timetable for interim meetings and deadlines. Agree that your team manager can be 'tough' on anyone who holds things up.

There cannot be a crisis next week. My schedule is already full.

Henry Kissinger, former American Secretary of State, *New York Times Magazine* (1969)

Preparing a team presentation

Share out the content

Where a team is made up of specialists, each speaker will obviously deal with their own part of the topic. If you can choose which part you present on, again distribute the roles according to people's enthusiasm for them.

With horrible parts—'No one wants to talk about *that*!'—give the eventual 'volunteer' plenty of help and support.

Plan the presentation

Some presentations will have to follow a certain order; with others you will be able to choose the order in which people speak. When you have a choice, choose an order which gives the audience some variety and contrast. For example:

■ if someone is presenting a lot of figures, they should be followed by a speaker with lively visual aids;

■ let someone who has a light and cheery approach follow a more serious speaker.

You can also alternate the voices. Even variety in the gender of the speaker makes the presentation sound more interesting.

Work together well

Each person is likely to prepare their own part of the presentation separately, but it is essential to meet to assess how things are shaping up. You can also run through a detailed outline of what each person expects to say, and the visual aids they will use. This will avoid finding gaps and overlaps at a later stage.

Tip
The team may need to do a pattern diagram together, to help them all see the overall picture and content.

See page 24 for more about pattern diagrams

 Do!

be prepared to listen to others' viewpoints.

 Do!

be prepared to consider making changes.

Rehearsing the team

Tip
Make sure you rehearse the handovers from one speaker to the next, and the end of the presentation. In group presentations these are often a shambles.

Rehearsals are important for all presentations, but essential for team presentations because they allow everyone in the team to make sure that they

■ avoid gaps;

■ avoid repetitions;

■ have polished introductions;

■ practise smooth handovers;

■ make sure they know who sums up and closes;

■ know who is inviting and answering questions.

See Ch. 6, Rehearsing

Have a strong leader for the day

It's essential that, with a team presentation, you have a leader on the day. Their role is to:

■ start the day going with introductions;

See Ch. 3, Structuring, for how to begin and end

■ move things along from one speaker to the next, if the presenters are not doing that themselves;

See Ch. 10, Managing your presentation

■ ask for questions and decide who answers them;

■ close the presentation.

The leader will be the first person from your team to address the audience, so choose a really good speaker with plenty of personality and a strong voice.

The team leader may not be the same person as the team manager, and could be one of the people doing a presentation during the day.

Rehearse handovers

It's particularly important to rehearse the handovers. It's getting the handover right, and the start and end, which shows you really are a team and not a group of individuals each working independently and without cooperation. When you take over, thank the previous speaker.

Do!

rehearse inviting and answering questions as well.

The smooth handover

> Ann: I will now hand over to Paul who will explain the steps we need to go through to make the changeover.
>
> Paul: Thank you Ann. [*Then to the audience*] I would like to spend the next fifteen minutes talking you through . . .

Go into it with attack. This is a strong moment in the presentation. You have the attention of the audience. Keep hold of it with your energy and enthusiasm.

Do!

rehearse individually and together. Give each other constructive feedback on what is working well, and what could do with some improvement.

Know who will cope with emergencies

During your rehearsals you might want to decide who will step in if something goes wrong, such as the technology suddenly stopping. You want to avoid a muddle, with everyone rushing forward to come to the rescue.

It's also worth considering whether you need an understudy. You should check that at least two people have a copy of all the presentations and, if there's a lot relying on a successful event, you should decide who could cover for anyone who's stuck in traffic, or has suddenly fallen ill.

People who stray

During your rehearsals you may discover that one of your team tends to stray into someone else's territory. This is a big fear with group presentations, but in fact it doesn't happen very often. Nevertheless, you may need some advice for handling it.

If possible, put that speaker on last (where they can do no damage!). Otherwise, you need to tell them at rehearsals as soon as they are out of their area. Keep telling them and make them rehearse until they stop doing it.

If it happens unexpectedly on the day—for example, if someone interrupts with a question, there are more things you can do.

- Try to think of some additional points you could make.

- If appropriate add your own opinion or feelings.

- When you speak, acknowledge that there's some repetition, but make it sound like a real benefit for everyone.

- Remember, if you smile and remain looking confident, the audience may well think you planned it this way.

Handling questions as a team

Make sure you know who will invite questions, who will decide who answers each one, and who will wind up the day when the questions have finished.

It's worth spending time during one of your team rehearsals:

- working out all the questions that might be asked;

- deciding who will field each question.

Have a good idea of what you would say in answer to your own questions.

Never

stray into someone else's material when you are part of a team presentation. It puts them in an impossible situation. It's unfair, and unprofessional.

Coping with overlap

'As Bob has already explained . . .'

'To recap on what David said . . .'

'Your earlier question showed how interested you are in this area, so I think it is worth running through some of the main . . .'

See Ch.10, Managing your presentation, for how to deal with questions

Being a team on the day

Before you start

Arrive early, especially if you have a lot of technology to set up.

Work out who will sit where. Will each speaker move in turn to the centre? Will you have your own seat to return to, or will you take the nearest available space. If there's a panel seating arrangement, will the name plates get muddled if you change places?

Never look through your own notes while a colleague is presenting. Support the speaker by looking at them—and expect them to do the same for you.

During the presentation

When they are not presenting, the rest of the team should listen to what their colleagues are saying. If the team looks bored, why should the audience be interested? So, look at the speaker and look involved in what they are saying. React to them appropriately. If they are presenting figures, smile if they are good, nod seriously if they are bad. And laugh gently at any comic comments. Yes, you have heard it before at rehearsals (and still find it amusing!).

You can glance to the audience from time to time to show you are in touch with them, with a knowing 'So what do you think of that' look.

At the end

It's particularly tempting for a team to forget that they are still presenting all the time they are within sight of the audience. Save your rejoicing shouts of 'Didn't that go *well*! We're *bound* to get the contract!' until they are out of the way. (Of course it went well—you planned and rehearsed it all!)

9 | Presenting with visual aids

Important

See Ch. 4, Choosing
and preparing visual
aids; Ch. 7, Giving
your presentation;
Ch. 10, Managing
your presentation

Remember!
You are your most
important visual aid.
Look calm, confident,
and 'the part'—then
any other visual aids
will add to your
performance, not
detract from it.

Top tip
concentrate on the
audience, not the
visuals. Every
moment of lost eye
contact is one of lost
communication.

Keep on presenting

It is impossible to over-emphasize the fact that your visual aids are not a substitute for communication. They are there to help you, and your audience. They are for clarifying complex information and adding a pictorial or diagrammatic element to the spoken word. Otherwise excellent presenters often 'fall apart' when they use visual aids because they try to let them carry the message.

Follow the basic principles of giving your presentation, to help ensure that visuals are aids, rather than deterrents, and make sure they do not overpower your presentation.

- Keep facing forward, even if the visual is being projected to the area behind you.

- Maintain your upright posture, so that you look and sound good.

- Make sure your face remains animated.

- Don't let the visuals draw attention from you.

- Project your voice and personality even more than usual.

- Don't let the visuals sap your energy, concentration, or focus.

  AND

- If you are using visual aids, you must rehearse.

Presenting with PowerPoint

More than any other visual aid, PowerPoint tends to draw the attention of the audience away from the speaker, which breaks the speaker–audience relationship. You need to inject energy to prevent this happening.

1. Take your presentation with you on disc and/or CD—with a back-up too.

2. Have a fall-back plan, such as OHP foils, so that you can still present if the technology does not work.

3. Be prepared to present with just *you* as the visual aid.

4. Arrive at least 45 minutes early if you have to set up the PowerPoint presentation—and always assume there will be some setting up to do.

5. Make friends with any technical experts on site.

6. Set up the room so that everyone can see the screen.

7. Ensure the screen-saver is turned off or it may switch in while you are speaking.

8. When presenting, concentrate on your audience, not the screen.

9. Don't check the image each time you change slides: what is on the laptop or monitor is also on the screen.

10. Let your audience look at each slide, then inject energy to bring attention back to you. This moves the focus between you and the screen, as appropriate.

11. Remember, people won't listen and read at the same time. If showing something complex, allow time for studying it. When about half the audience is looking back to you, draw the rest back: 'As you can see . . .'

12. When projecting onto an electronic whiteboard, do not draw attention to points by touching the screen, which may make it move to the next slide.

Tip
If you are operating the presentation from your laptop, elevate it so that you can change screens without stooping.

Pointing
Be careful with laser pointers. They amplify nervous hands.
- Point steadily, not with a 'wiggle'.
- Don't point the laser at the audience.
- Consider using a traditional, telescopic pointer.

Tip
To keep people focused on you use your
- voice
- face
- body
- personality
- excitement
- energy
- enthusiasm.

Presenting with a flip chart

1. Make sure there is plenty of paper—and that none of the sheets have already been used.

2. Avoid scrunched up sheets, which look messy.

3. Put a squiggle in the corner of a page towards the back of the pad. Then you can slow down if you start to run out of paper.

4. Give the back leg of the chart a gentle 'kick' to ensure it's fully extended.

5. Check you have enough pens, and that they work.

6. Write in a dark colour, with letters at least 5 cm high. Use other colours for highlights.

7. If you are right handed, stand with the flip chart on your left. If left handed, stand with it on your right. Then you can write without moving your body too much.

8. You do not need to be an artist to do a quick sketch. Practise what you might want to draw.

9. Don't talk and write at the same time: you will have your back to the audience, so no eye contact. You will also be less audible.

10. Turn the pages completely to avoid building a strange paper sculpture at the back of the chart, which eventually makes it impossible to turn the pages.

11. If you expect to return to a page, turn over the corner or apply a small adhesive sticker, so that you can find the page easily.

12. Never point to words on the flip chart with such enthusiasm that you hit it with a hand or pointer. The effect is comic—and in extreme cases the flip chart will fall over!

Tip

It's best to take your own flip chart pens. That way you can be sure you have the colours you want— and a type of pen you can write neatly with.

T is for technique

Make sure your flip chart technique is good. So that you don't write and speak at the same time, tell yourself that what you must do is

T

*   **Talk** with the group
*   **Turn** to write
*   **Touch** the chart— that is, write on it.

Presenting with an overhead projector

1. Place the projector so people can see it. If the picture is not square, tilt the projector using a book (not this one!), or whatever is to hand. Or, tilt the screen.

2. Place the projector so that the picture will be the right size. To make it bigger, move it further away. To make it smaller, move it closer.

3. Clean the screen if it's grubby. Put a coin onto the screen to help you get a really sharp focus using the large knob near the magnifying lens.

4. Use the OHP controls to remove the brown/blue effect from the image edges to get a clear, white screen.

5. Organize the area with space for the foils you will use, the one you are showing, those you have shown, and for interleaving sheets if you have used them.

6. Stand where you do not block the screen.

7. Put each foil squarely in place. It appears on the screen the same way up as on the projector, so no need to check.

8. Change foils smoothly, sliding one off and the next one on to avoid the audience looking at a blank screen.

9. Avoid masking parts of the text and then revealing it slowly. Audiences find it irritating. If you want to reveal text in bits, show the whole screen first, then cover the parts you are not dealing with. Better still, avoid making the foil too busy in the first place.

10. Do not walk between the projector and the screen, unless you want the image projected onto your body.

11. Draw attention to a point by placing a pencil on the glass, rather than pointing.

12. Avoid looking at the glass of the machine too much as the bright light can leave you dazzled.

 Do!

take with you
- spare bulbs
- an extension lead
- a damp cloth.

Warning!
If you move the machine once the bulb is hot, it may 'blow'.

Tip
Practise your sliding change-over technique: it's easy once you get the movement flowing.

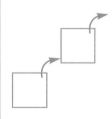

Tip
Do not use a round pencil as the pointer—it may roll off. Choose one which is hexagonal.

10 | Managing your presentation

See Part B,
On the day checklist

Arrive early

You must arrive early. If you arrive early you are far less likely to be nervous and flustered during the presentation. You will be able to familiarize yourself with your performance space and arrange things the way you want them. You will be able to say a few words to test out the room's acoustic. And you will be able to take a few quiet moments to get your thoughts in order and do a little deep breathing to help you relax.

Allow time for the journey to go wrong, and the room not to be set up the way you want when you arrive.

When others are early

It's distracting when people arrive while you are still setting up your presentation and trying to relax. If possible, put a note on the door to say when the room will be 'open'. If people 'barge in' tell them where they can find teas, coffees, etc. If they insist on staying, take control. Say who you are, then:

> Forgive me if I ignore you for the moment, but I still have some setting up to do.

They *may* take the hint and go!

Remember
If using visual aids, allow plenty of time to set things up. The more complex the visual aids, the longer they will take.

Room layouts

The room layout may be a 'given': you may have to work with what you get. If you can choose the way the room is set up, your decision will affect your relationship with your audience and your presentation. But always remember that, despite your request beforehand, the room may not be set up as you expected when you arrive, so allow time to move the furniture yourself if the layout is essential to your success.

If presenting one-to-one across a desk, make sure you do not invade your listener's 'territory' by assuming you can place your papers on their desk.

U-shape

The U-shape (below left) is the best shape for maintaining contact with up to 20 people. You can see them all, and can walk up the centre of the U, and round its edges if you want. It's a good layout if you hope to involve people with your presentation, and with each other, and if you want them to ask questions or discuss issues.

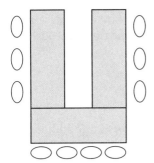

Boardroom

For presentations, the boardroom (above right) is the least favourable layout. It works with up to 20 people, but is more formal than the U-shape. It is uncomfortable to work with because, as the presenter, you have little ability to move, and it's virtually impossible to maintain eye contact with those to your immediate left and right. However, people will be willing to discuss and become involved when you use this layout.

School room

Individual desks (below left) can work for up to 40 people, but as any teacher will tell you, keeping control of the group is hard. You can't really be in touch with both the back and front of the room. If people are seated in pairs they may have more contact with each other than with you. They will be more involved and questioning if they can see each other.

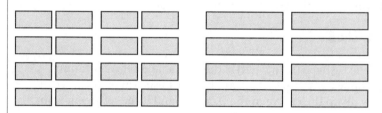

Theatre

See Ch. 7, Giving
your presentation

The theatre layout (above right) is rather formal. It works for any number of people—literally thousands—but they will listen rather than question. In smaller lecture theatres you can use the width of the room, and walk up and down the aisle if that suits your style.

Cabaret

Mischievous mikes

With theatre or cabaret layout you may need a microphone, and they can be tricky. Like children, mikes always seem to 'hear' things they shouldn't. If a mike is near you, do not utter a syllable that you wouldn't say face-to-face to your grandmother, your boss, or your tutor!

The cabaret layout (below) can work for very large audiences and is often used at lunches, dinners, and other semi-formal occasions. As the event is likely to be friendly—and may involve a fair amount of alcohol—this layout demands an enormous amount of energy from the speaker. If you are an extrovert speaker, use the space by walking round the room—though you may need a lapel microphone.

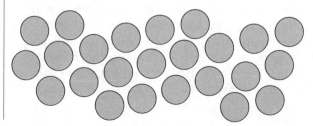

Handouts

If you provide handouts, when should you distribute them?

Before

If you give people the handouts before the presentation, you will find it much harder to maintain contact with them as they will have their heads down most of the time.

People will read ahead so you lose the ability to build a case or argument. In certain situations, someone may even try to 'jump' you ahead to a later part of what you plan to say: 'I see on page 15 that . . .' Or they may not bother staying to listen.

Provide handouts beforehand if people need to make notes. If you are using PowerPoint, you can create handouts of the screens, with lines for your listeners' notes.

During

In small groups, you can distribute handouts as you go along, in a series of sets. This allows people to make notes, but limits the jumping ahead they do. Make sure distributing papers is a change of pace, not a time-consuming muddle. And make the process foolproof: staple pages, use coloured dividers, and if appropriate consecutive page numbers.

After

If you plan to distribute handouts at the end, let people know how detailed they will be so that they do not take unnecessary notes. Remember, finishing by distributing papers can be a bit lame—and some people may have to leave before the end.

> ### At the door
> Consider putting handouts by the door for people to collect when they leave.

Do you need them?

Use handouts when
- you want to create a lasting impression
- people need an accurate record of what you said
- people may need to be referred to certain facts or points
- the presentation is part of a 'learning experience'.

Handouts at the outset can be good in one-to-one, across-the-desk presentations.

See page 70 for more on handouts

 Do!

consider providing handouts on CD or on a user-group website. This is becoming accepted—and even expected—in business presentations.

Handling questions

A great advantage of presentations is that they provide two-way communication. Indeed, the main reason for presenting is often to give the audience a chance to ask questions.

Presenters vary in their attitude to questions. Some thoroughly enjoy them, because they sense that they are really communicating with the audience. Others dislike them, because they feel they have less control over what is happening, and fear that they could be asked questions about an area in which they are not particularly strong.

Inviting questions

The phrase that we all know well—and the one that most of us resort to—is 'Has anyone got any questions?' However, this may not be the most appropriate phrase to use because it contains a slight hint of 'Who is so stupid that they haven't understood some of that and needs me to say it again?'

A better, though longer, way of requesting questions would sound more inviting.

> I have given you an overview of the situation, and I am sure some of you might like more information about some areas, so who would like to begin with the first question?

You can even point the direction of the first question.

> . . . For example, I wonder whether some of you might like more information about the marketing plans that will be supporting these changes.

When the question arrives

Do not change character when you answer questions. Some presenters only smile, relax, and become 'themselves' when they hear the first question. When that happens, the presentation suddenly comes to life.

Remember

Someone may need to interrupt you with a question. If you use a term they don't know, such as SLR, they will be lost without a definition. (SLR is a single-lens reflex camera!)

Other presenters clam up when it comes to questions, becoming rigid and nervous, because they feel they are in uncharted waters and fear what the questions might lead to.

There are a few simple guidelines for answering questions.

Welcome the question

Acknowledge that you have 'received' the question. The phrase 'That's a very good question' is so associated with squirming politicians that the audience may chuckle. Try 'Good point!' or even a thoughtful: 'Mmmm—good question'.

Repeat and clarify

You may need to repeat the question if the room is large, or if the questioner has a quiet voice.

If the question is unclear, ask the questioner what they mean.

Only in desperate situations

If a questioner goes on and on (and on, and on, and on) and is obviously making a point rather than asking a question, break your eye contact with them.

This usually makes it harder for them to keep talking, but it's bad manners. Only do it on the rarest of occasions.

> Are you referring to our goals over this season, or over the calendar year?

Spot the question!

Some people never get round to asking the question—they just present an opinion. Think hard about your response while they are talking, and bring it back to a positive.

> Thank you for filling us in on what is happening in this field in Germany. Next question?

Answering the question

- Keep the answer brief.

- Answer the question mainly to the questioner. If the answer has to be longish, make brief eye contact with the rest of the room occasionally during the answer, so that they feel included in the information.

- Check back that you have answered the question to the questioner's satisfaction.

Tricky situations

Golden rules

- Don't change your manner, body language, or expression.

- Don't 'back away' from the question, by taking a small step backwards!

- Do take a step forward to 'welcome' the question—that will surprise people!

No questions?

Don't be miserable if there are no questions, even if you were hoping for some. Instead, turn it into a positive point, repeat your main message and retreat. (And keep smiling!)

> No questions? In that case, I'm glad that I've managed to make the process clear. I would just like to repeat that I truly consider that this is the best way forward, and that if we are to start implementing the changes this year, a decision needs to be made by the end of this month. Thank your for your time.

Swan through it
Remember the swan? See page 82.

Tip
Reinforce your main message after the last question, so that your audience remembers what you want them to remember. And then depart with dignity.

Avoid this
Speakers who are concerned about not having any questions often get a colleague or friend to ask one. It normally sounds contrived so avoid doing it.

Too many questions (from one person)

It's reasonable to allow someone one supplementary question, but after that it's becoming a conversation between the two of you. Unless the person has particular power or authority, don't allow a third question. Instead say that, as they have a particular interest, you will talk to them in the break.

You've already said it

They dropped out mentally for a moment! Don't say 'I've already explained that!' Do say: 'I'm sorry I didn't make that clear. The situation is . . .' and repeat the point *briefly!*

You don't know the answer

In the workplace you aren't normally expected to know the answer to everything. If you should have anticipated interest in the point, apologize for not knowing the answer. Then:

◼ if appropriate, say you will find out and get back to the questioner if they let you have contact details;

◼ refer the question to someone else in the audience—but only if they are expecting you to do so.

Students who don't know . . .

If you are a student and don't know the answer, admit it. Otherwise, you can 'dig a hole for yourself' that just gets deeper and deeper.

You cannot 'make things up': with factual questions: there is only one right answer. In opinion-based questions you may be able to 'lead' the questions elsewhere.

> I don't know what Shaw wrote about his emotional response to poetry, but I did find his comments on music . . .

Maybe not
If you want to stop a flow of questions don't be tempted by the phrase used by old Father William (as much as you might want to!):

*I have
answered three
questions, and
that is enough
. . . Be off, or
I'll kick you
downstairs!*

Lewis Carroll, *Alice's Adventures in Wonderland* (1865)

Never despair.

Horace, *Epistles* (65–8 BCE)

Students take note
If you get asked tricky questions, it doesn't spell trouble. Your examiner is giving you an opportunity to demonstrate your knowledge—not trying to catch you out.

The insecure, egotists, and show-offs

Speakers are occasionally given a tough time by an audience, but it's rare and presenters usually know when they are going into a potentially 'dangerous' situation, such as dealing with bad news. However, despite all your planning, you could find that someone in the audience has an 'agenda' you did not know about. They may be insecure, have an ego problem, or want to show off. There are ways of coping.

> **Q:** Why do we have to install this new system?

Throw the question back to the person who asked it

> **A:** We don't. But I'd be interested to consider which accounting system you believe we should adopt.

> **Q:** We have tried this before, and it didn't work then. Why should it work now?

You could put this question up for general discussion.

> **A:** It will work now partly because the market has changed. But I'd be interested to hear how others here believe we can improve retention figures in the short term?

> **Q:** To what extent is this product biodegradable at a level that will be acceptable to new European legislation?

This questioner seems to need to show off their knowledge so flatter them—and demonstrate your own knowledge.

> **A:** ... I didn't mention this before because I wanted to avoid such a high level of technical detail, and as you know it does not affect cost.

To avoid shocks
- Find out who will be in the audience.
- Think about their interests, concerns, and feelings.
- Address the issues in your presentation.

 Do!

stay calm if you get a tricky question.

 Don't!

show what you are really feeling!

Remember
The rest of your audience may feel as irritated with a questioner as you do, and will admire you for coping.

Managing time

You must keep to the given timeframe. If people ask you to speak for 20 minutes, followed by ten minutes of questions, that's what you must provide—not a 30-minute talk.

If you fail to keep to time it not only looks unprofessional, it also causes all sorts of problems for other people. If you end early, the next speaker may not be quite ready to take over. If you talk for too long, you will cause a knock-on effect for everyone present for the rest of the day. If you talk much too long, people will—quite rightly—get up and walk out. Students giving presentations as part of their assessed work will often be marked down for going over time.

Reading aloud
One page of double-spaced paper takes around two minutes to read aloud. As minor changes to pace or density of the text can affect this timing dramatically, you must check the timing when you rehearse.

If others do not keep to time, you may be asked to get things back on schedule by speaking for longer, or for less time.

Always plan how you would cope.

• Take additional material with you that you could use if needed, such as a case history, or extra examples.
• Decide which parts of your presentation you could drop and still keep the flow of what you are saying. Mark your notes accordingly.

How to keep to time

The only way to keep to time is to rehearse your presentation, using the visual aids you plan to use.

If you cannot rehearse with the visuals, allow an additional 5-10 seconds for each one you show. If you are showing six, that will add about a minute to your presentation.

If for some reason you cannot go through your presentation out loud, you are taking enormous risks. But to help you keep to time, go through it really, really slowly in your head. You can 'think' words much faster than you can say them. Remember to allow for some pauses in your speech, and remember that you could be interrupted.

See page 73

A few reminders

See Ch. 2, Preparing, and checklists in Part B

1. Never forget that managing your presentation will be easiest if you have prepared.

See page 91 for more about visualizing

2. Make sure you think through and plan for things that could go wrong—and then visualize how successful your presentation is going to be.

See Ch. 6, Rehearsing

3. Don't regard rehearsing as an optional extra: it's a transforming exercise.

See page 82

4. Remember the swan—be serene on the surface, but inject energy to keep the momentum going.

See Ch. 7, Giving your presentation, for more about nerves and appearances, and there is more advice in Part B

5. Recognize that elements of your presentation will be judged on rather superficial points. So make sure you:

   ■ stay calm and in control—then people will think you are;

   ■ look the part—appearances count;

   ■ keep to time—it's a sign of professionalism.

6. Concentrate on the fact that you are communicating, not on the fact that you are presenting.

And finally . . .

See the magic circle on page 83

Enjoy the experience. Remember to smile. If you do, you really will enjoy the presentation more—and so will your audience.

Good luck!

Part B: Reference section
Contents

The presenter's toolkit

You will need:

- [ ] notes
- [ ] visual aids
- [ ] duplicate of materials on CD, disc, or both
- [ ] timer, if not using your watch
- [ ] directions to the venue
- [ ] contact name and number.

✘ Don't!

rely on being able to borrow leads, paper, and other bits and pieces at the venue.

You may need:

- [ ] flip chart pens
- [ ] mini-toolkit for screwdrivers, etc.
- [ ] bottle of water
- [ ] pointer
- [ ] adhesive tape and labels
- [ ] paper and pencils for note-taking (in case it is needed)
- [ ] books, brochures, or samples you will refer to.

And of course you definitely need

- [ ] a well prepared and rehearsed presentation
- [ ] a large bag of self-confidence.

Planning: the audience

Checklists

See Ch. 2,
Preparing

For a perfect, ideal presentation, you should be able to answer 'yes' to all these questions.

☐ Have you thought about your audience in every possible way?

Do you know . . .

☐ what the audience already knows about the subject?

☐ whether they have strong opinions on the subject?

☐ what they hope for from the time they spend listening?

☐ what their concerns are?

☐ what communication methods they prefer (listen, discuss)?

☐ what kind of argument will convince them (numeric, people points, logic)?

☐ who is the decision maker?

☐ whether they will be there willingly?

☐ what sort of concentration span they will have?

☐ how many people will be there?

☐ whether any of the audience may have weak English?

And finally . . .

☐ will anyone else be talking to them on the subject?

Planning: the content

For a perfect presentation, you should work your way through all these questions.

See Ch. 2, Preparing, and Ch. 3, Structuring

☐ Do you know what you want to happen as a result of the presentation? (Your aim)

☐ Have you tied what *you* want into the interests of your audience? (Your message)

☐ Have you kept to a few points, but supported them in a variety of ways?

☐ Is the content pitched at an appropriate level for your audience?

☐ Have you covered all points and angles (at least in your thoughts, even if some of the material is not included in your talk)?

☐ Have you structured your presentation in a readily understood way, so that you do not make too many demands on your audience?

☐ Have you brought variety into what you are saying, by expressing it in different ways (numbers, anecdotes)?

☐ Have you found an interesting, and attention-grabbing way to start?

See Ch.10, Managing your presentation

☐ Have you remembered to make the ending as strong as possible and used it as a way to reinforce your message?

☐ Have you decided whether you want to be asked questions, and whether you are expecting them at the end or as you go along?

☐ Have you decided whether you need to use handouts, and if so, when you will distribute them?

Planning: you the presenter

For a perfect presentation, you should work your way through all these questions.

☐ Are you confident about the knowledge and experience you bring to the presentation?

☐ If there are aspects of your specialist subject you are uncertain about, are there people or publications that will help you?

☐ Have you built the strength of your voice by singing in the shower?

☐ Have you checked your posture in front of a mirror to see how confident you can look?

☐ Have you done some reading aloud to practise using your voice in an interesting way?

☐ Have you decided what you will wear, and checked that it is clean, ironed, and has all the buttons in place?

☐ Do you believe that smiling really can make you feel much, much more confident?

☐ Are you certain you know how to use the visual aids you have decided to use?

☐ Have you checked that the venue can supply all you need in the way of hardware, software, leads, and power supplies?

☐ Have you checked how the venue will be laid out, and whether you can change it if it is not as you want it?

☐ Have you checked all your handouts and visual aids for accuracy, order, and completeness?

☐ Have your rehearsed your presentation aloud, and timed it?

Checklists

If there are areas you feel less than confident about, build your skills. Refer in particular to Ch. 7, Giving your presentation, and Ch. 9, Presenting with visual aids.

See the presenter's toolkit, page 122

On the day

Before you leave

Remember!
Alcohol and presentations do not go together. Wait— and give yourself a treat later.

☐ Have you checked the time, date, and place?

☐ Have you got your notes?

☐ Have you got your visual aids?

☐ Have you got your handouts?

See Ch. 9,
Presenting with visual aids

☐ Have you everything else you may possibly need?

When you arrive

☐ Find the power sockets if you are using PowerPoint, slides, or an OHP.

☐ Find the light switch.

☐ Check the fire exits.

☐ Find the toilets!

☐ Arrange the room.

☐ Set up your performing space.

☐ Set up your visual aids.

☐ Make sure that all the technology works properly.

See Ch. 3,
Structuring your presentation

☐ Make sure you have room to move, and a place to put everything you need.

☐ Check for interruptions, such as fire alarms and tea.

At the end

☐ If you are escorted from the premises, remember you are still presenting until you are out of sight.

Starting and ending

At the start

See Ch. 3, Structuring

☐ Greet your audience.

☐ Welcome your audience.

☐ Thank them for attending.

☐ Give your name clearly.

☐ Give your authority for speaking.

☐ Tell them how long you will be speaking.

☐ Say if you want questions at the end, or during the presentation.

☐ Tell them whether they should take notes.

See Ch. 4, Choosing and preparing visual aids, and Ch. 9, Presenting with visual aids

☐ Say whether there are handouts.

☐ Let them know about fire exits.

☐ Tell them about scheduled breaks.

☐ Mention mobile phones, if appropriate.

☐ Give your talk in outline.

At the end

☐ Invite and answer questions.

☐ Distribute handouts.

☐ Repeat your message.

☐ If appropriate, repeat what should happen next.

☐ Repeat that you will follow up any points that have arisen.

☐ Thank your audience for their time.

Checklists

Working with PowerPoint or slides

Preparing

You should be able to answer 'yes' to these questions:

☐ Does PowerPoint *support* the message, not *give* it?

☐ Do you have copies on CD, or a duplicate disc?

☐ Are your slides visual, rather than wordy?

☐ Does the venue have the facilities you need?

☐ Is each visual clear, uncluttered, and easily legible?

☐ Have you kept it down to one visual every two minutes?

☐ Are your slides numbered in the bottom left?

☐ Are you completely familiar with the software?

☐ Will you be able to cope without PowerPoint?

☐ Do you have a fall-back plan, such as OHP transparencies of your presentation?

☐ Is the software at the venue compatible with yours?

☐ Do you have a selection of spare leads and cables?

☐ Will you have access to the room in time to set up?

On the day

☐ Make sure you are comfortable with the room layout.

☐ Make sure everyone can see the screen.

☐ When presenting, allow time for people to absorb any complex slides.

☐ Don't lose eye contact with your audience.

When?

Use PowerPoint if
• people expect it
• the audience is large
• you want to use special effects
• you need to show video clips.

Choose slides if
• you need clear definition, such as photos of buildings or surgical procedures.

Remember!

Always allow yourself plenty of time if you need to set up PowerPoint.

See Ch. 4, Choosing and preparing visual aids, and Ch. 9, Presenting with visual aids

Working with a flip chart

Preparing

- ☐ Find out what type of chart is available.

- ☐ Prepare or 'ghost' pages if you need to.

- ☐ Obtain a range of working pens in plenty of colours.

On the day

Before you start

- ☐ Try to obtain a free-standing chart if only a wall-mounted one is provided.

- ☐ Position the chart so that everyone can see it.

- ☐ Make sure the rear foot is fully extended.

- ☐ Make sure you have good pens in a range of colours.

- ☐ Check that the chart has plenty of clean paper.

- ☐ Mark a page near the end with a 'warning' sign.

- ☐ Place the chart on the side away from your writing hand.

- ☐ 'Ghost' any charts or diagrams and mark the page.

When presenting

- ☐ Avoid speaking and writing at the same time.

- ☐ If you think you may need to return to a page, turn up the corner or use a sticker.

- ☐ Abbreviate long words to save time.

- ☐ Write in letters about 5 cm high.

- ☐ Turn each page completely.

See Ch. 4, Choosing and preparing visual aids, and Ch. 9, Presenting with visual aids

When?

Choose a flip chart when
- you want to be informal
- you want to involve the group
- people need to watch complex calculations appear slowly.

- Talk

- Turn

- Touch

Working with an overhead projector (OHP)

Preparing

☐ On pre-prepared overheads use a dark colour on a light ground.

☐ Use lettering which is at least a 20 point typeface.

☐ Put overheads in card or plastic frames for easy handling.

☐ If you do not have frames, interleave with sheets of paper to prevent sticking.

☐ Take spare bulbs and extension leads with you.

See Ch. 4, Choosing and preparing visual aids, and Ch. 9, Presenting with visual aids

On the day

☐ Set up the OHP so that the screen is visible to all.

☐ Organize your performance area, with space for overheads you have yet to use, those you have used, and interleaving pages.

☐ Clean the screen and focus the picture.

☐ Find a comfortable position from which to present and where you do not block the screen.

When?
Choose an OHP when
● it's the only option available
● you want to prepare material
● you want to be informal.

When presenting

☐ Slide one overhead off as you slide the next one on.

☐ Blank out the screen to prevent leaving a dazzling light in the room.

☐ Point by laying a hexagonal pencil on the screen, rather than using a finger or pointer.

Dealing with questions

Asking for questions

☐ Invite the question: 'Who would like more detail?'

See pages 114–19 for more about how to deal with questions, including the tricky ones

Answering questions

☐ Clarify the question if you need to.

☐ Repeat the question if it may not have been audible to the audience.

☐ Answer mainly to the questioner—but to others too.

☐ Keep your answer brief.

☐ Check back that you have answered the question.

☐ Allow just one supplementary question.

☐ Move on.

☐ Reinforce the main message at the end of the questions.

Tricky questions

☐ Plan in advance to avoid surprises.

☐ Do not panic.

☐ Remember the questioner may have an 'agenda'.

☐ Do not change your body language.

☐ Take a step toward the question, rather than away from it.

☐ Answer briefly and concisely.

☐ Keep looking positive.

Team presentations

See Ch. 8, Team presentations

Before the presentation

☐ Share out the roles.

☐ Draw up a timetable.

☐ Hold regular meetings.

☐ Rehearse separately.

☐ Know who will

   ○ introduce the presentation;

   ○ introduce the speakers;

   ○ move on from one speaker to the next;

   ○ request questions;

   ○ decide who answers;

   ○ bring the presentation to a close.

☐ Rehearse together.

☐ Give each other feedback.

During the presentation

☐ Look at the person speaking.

☐ Listen with interest.

☐ Do not trespass on each other's territory.

Presenting one-to-one

Presentations made to just one or two people are frequently given 'across the desk' rather than standing, for example when presenting a business plan to a bank manager, or giving a short talk to introduce your thesis to an examiner.

☐ Remember, first impressions count, so enter the room with confidence.

☐ Enter the room with your right hand free, so that you can get off to a good start with a handshake.

☐ When you enter the room, wait to be shown where to sit: you don't want to take the tutor's chair.

☐ Still use notes: a flow chart or pattern diagram might feel more natural than cards.

See pages 66–69

☐ Avoid putting papers on the desk between you and your 'audience'. Your listener could consider you are 'invading their space'.

☐ Only accept coffee or tea if you are sure you can cope with the cup and saucer along with everything else.

☐ Watch your body language and make sure you don't 'droop' in your seat, particularly if you have your notes on your lap. Sit back, and up.

☐ Make eye contact, but when presenting one-to-one, you will need to change where you look occasionally, or you will seem to be 'staring each other out'. Glance elsewhere, but not the ceiling or the floor.

☐ Remember, you will still need to inject energy—especially if the bank manager has a desk the size of a tennis court. But you can scale things down from what you would do to a really large group.

☐ Make a good exit. Your presentation ends when you are out of the room, out of the building, and out of sight.

Preparing in a hurry

Do!

get together everything you need and shut yourself away in a quiet place to prepare.

Do!

invest your time in:
● thinking
● preparing notes
● rehearsing.

Don't!

lose valuable time preparing visual aids.

Although you should ideally have plenty of time to prepare and practise your presentation, there may be times when you have to put your talk together in a rush.

The P O W E R plan will help you prepare when time is short.

P lan
Consider your audience and aims.
Do a quick pattern diagram.
Select which parts to use.

O rganize
Put your information under headings.
Devise a straight-forward structure.

W rite
Write your prompt cards or other notes.
Rewrite any notes that look messy.

E dit
Delete unnecessary information.
Keep it as simple as possible.

R ehearse
Go through your notes.
If you have time, say the presentation aloud.

Working across languages and cultures

If you have to present overseas, or to people from overseas in your own country, think about these extra points.

What you say

☐ Be meticulous about introducing topics, giving part-way summaries, and summing up.

☐ Avoid colloquialisms which may be taken literally.

☐ Use visual support to clarify.

☐ Use a straightforward and jargon-free vocabulary.

You'll do what, why?

I'll kick off straight away, without beating about the bush. I realize this throws some of you in the deep end, but it's better than going round the houses, and we cannot leave this issue on the back burner any longer.

How you say it

☐ Never assume that people understand spoken language as well as they do when it is written down.

☐ Speak clearly and slowly.

☐ Recognize that people subconsciously lip read, so moving your lips in a more pronounced way will aid understanding.

☐ If you have a strong accent, bear this in mind.

Magic moments
Pausing regularly will transform your audience's ability to take in what you say.

135

Working with an interpreter

☐ Keep it simple, and talk in complete sentences.

☐ Remember, your presentation will take twice as long.

☐ Work out what you plan to do about visual aids. You should really show them twice. Work with your interpreter to know how he or she will indicate the need to change visual. Remember, impact will be lost second time around.

Note

With two minutes of speech, a translator will be able to give a summary of what you have said, not a direct translation. If you want a detailed translation, you will need to pause at the end of each sentence.

☐ If you have to use technical or specialized vocabulary, let the agency providing the interpreter know beforehand so that they can send the most appropriate person.

☐ When presenting, speak for a couple of minutes and then stop for them to interpret. While they are interpreting, look interested, sharing your attention between the interpreter and your audience.

☐ With simultaneous interpretation, when the audience hears you through headphones, you have an easier time. But your interpreter still needs complete sentences to work with.

Body language

Most cultures will make allowances, but do seek advice about local customs beforehand.

Reaction (or lack thereof)

Be aware that in some cultures people simply do not interact with the speaker. The fact that you are not getting facial signals from your audience does not necessarily mean they dislike what you are saying, or do not understand you.

A script prepared for reading

See pages 60-61 for working with a script

I think it's <u>important</u> to look at the impact that <u>home working</u> could have on the <u>environment.</u>

Underlining for emphasis.

If we take a <u>simplistic</u> view, we would say that home working must improve things./If everyone worked form hone one day a week there would be 20% fewer cars on the road, and <u>more space</u> on trains and tubes - which just might attract more passengers, and so one. But what about those home workers?//If there were only <u>10,000</u> of them that would be <u>10,000 extra</u> <u>homes being lit and heated.</u> The sums are not so straight-forward as they seem. (PAUSE FOR THOUGHT)

A slash to show a short pause.

A double slash to show a slightly longer pause.

A long pause at the paragraph end for the final point to sink in.

/There are other environmental issues as well//Unscrupulous employers,(and there are plenty of those about,)distribute dangerous chemicals to homes which <u>simply</u> <u>do</u> <u>not</u> <u>have</u> <u>the</u> <u>correct</u> <u>means</u> <u>for</u> <u>disposing</u> <u>of</u> <u>them.</u> The little odd bit of this and that poured down a domestic sink will go unnoticed. But if those manufacturers attempted to dispose of the <u>same</u> <u>total</u> <u>amount</u> of chemicals at their own sites, they <u>simply</u> <u>would</u> <u>not</u> <u>be</u> <u>allowed</u> <u>to</u> <u>do</u> <u>it.</u> (PAUSE FOR THOUGHT)

//There are other.....

An upward sign as a fresh energy reminder at paragraph start.

Bracket to remind the reader to lower the tone of the voice.

Consecutive words underlined for slow, emphatic pace.

Dealing with nerves

Calm your mind to feel more confident

☐ Recognize that nerves are natural energy, which you can channel into your presentation.

☐ Prepare thoroughly: nothing makes you feel more confident than knowing what you plan to say and do.

See Ch. 7, Giving your presentation

☐ Rehearse and rehearse.

☐ Visualize success.

nerves
↓
adrenalin
↓
energy → fear
↓   ↓
present

☐ Remember, smiling creates 'feel good' hormones.

☐ Take two or three slow, deep breaths before you start.

☐ Concentrate on your audience, rather than yourself.

Cope with your body

Red in the face?
If you tend to go pink when you present, concentrating on the audience rather than your pinkness can help. There are also homeopathic and herbal remedies that can help. Speak to a specialist for details.

☐ Relax your knees to prevent trembling legs.

☐ Sit palms up to avoid sweaty hands.

☐ Lower your shoulders.

☐ Breathe slowly and fully to relax your breathing.

Cope with your voice

☐ Pause to give yourself time to breathe.

☐ Relax your jaw (and think of lemons) to avoid a dry mouth.

How to choose a course

When you have mastered the principles of presenting, your next step might be to go on a presentations skills course. There's nothing like standing and giving a presentation to find out how well you come across to a group. There are many, many courses available, from evening classes, to in-house and one-to-one coaching. If you want to keep improving your skills, here are some questions to ask before signing up.

See Ch. 6, Rehearsing your presentation

How many people will be taking part in the course?
If more than eight people are taking part, your involvement is likely to be quite low.

How many presentations will you give?
There's no ideal answer, but be aware that on some courses not all participants get to present, and it's the ones who need practice—the most nervous ones—who don't volunteer.

How long are the presentations?
If all the presentations are just a few minutes long, think again. Longer presentations—ten or fifteen minutes—create different issues for the speaker, such as waning energy.

What does the course focus on?
Some courses are keen on performance skills, but don't deal with tailoring for your audience, or structure.

Will you be videoed, and can you keep the video?
You may hate the idea, but you can learn an enormous amount just from seeing yourself on video. It's worth it!

Who will give feedback?
Ideally, you want feedback from an experienced tutor and from other members of the group.

Further reading and resources

Books

The Voice and the Actor, Cicely Berry (Virgin Publishing, 1997). This is a 'classic' on the voice which has been around for quite a few years, with good reason. Very readable advice on breathing, relaxation, a mass of voice exercises, and expert advice on voice production and use.

Clear Speech, Malcolm Morrison (A&C Black, 2001). A quick and easy guide to pronunciation, with practical exercises.

People Watching, Desmond Morris (Vintage, 2002). This book on body language was originally published some time ago, but is hard to surpass, particularly as it includes information about gestures overseas.

The Little Book of Courage, Sarah Quigley, Marilyn Shroyer (Conari Press, 1996). This book takes you through the three steps to overcoming anxiety: facing fear, feeling fear, and transforming fear.

Body Talk at Work, Judi James (Piatkus, 2001). How to use effective body language to boost your career.

Teach Yourself Alexander Technique, Richard Craze (Hodder & Stoughton, 2001). How to stand and move correctly to save your voice and reduce stress.

Quick Course in Microsoft PowerPoint 2000, Joyce Cox and Polly Urban (Microsoft Press, 1999). A reasonably priced step-by-step guide to creating a PowerPoint presentation.

One Step Ahead: Presenting Numbers, Tables, and Charts, Sally Bigwood and Melissa Spore, (Oxford University Press, 2003). More detailed advice on the best way to put numbers across to your audience.

One Step Ahead: Spelling, Robert Allen, (Oxford University Press, 2002). Useful advice, pointers, and lists for uncertain users of flip charts (or creators of any other visual aids).

Oxford Dictionaries of Quotations. Wonderful sources of quotations which will liven up any presentation. As well as a large book of general quotations and a dictionary of modern quotations, there are specialist books covering such subjects as humour and politics.

Web sites

The English Speaking Union (www.esu.org). An international organization which runs a variety of debating, public speaking events, and educational programmes for young people all over the world.

Toastmasters (www.toastmasters.org). A nationwide network of Toastmasters groups where members learn presentation skills for a short spell each week, for a number of weeks.

Index